HAVE CONSECRATED IT FAR ABO[VE]
OUR POOR POWER TO ADD OR DET[RACT.]
THE WORLD WILL LITTLE NOT[E] NOR
LONG REMEMBER WHAT WE SAY HERE
BUT IT CAN NEVER FORGET WHAT THEY
DID HERE · IT IS FOR US THE LIVING
RATHER TO BE DEDICATED HERE TO
THE UNFINISHED WORK WHICH THEY
WHO FOUGHT HERE HAVE THUS FAR
SO NOBLY ADVANCED · IT IS RATHER FOR
US TO BE HERE DEDICATED TO THE
GREAT TASK REMAINING BEFORE US~
THAT FROM THESE HONORED DEAD
WE TAKE INCREASED DEVOTION TO
THAT CAUSE FOR WHICH THEY GAVE THE
LAST FULL MEASURE OF DEVOTION~
THAT WE HERE HIGHLY RESOLVE THAT
THESE DEAD SHALL NOT HAVE DIED IN
VAIN~THAT THIS NATION UNDER GOD
SHALL HAVE A NEW BIRTH OF FREEDOM~
AND THAT GOVERNMENT OF THE PEOPLE
BY THE PEOPLE FOR THE PEOPLE SHALL
NOT PERISH FROM THE EARTH ·

ETCHED IN STONE

ETCHED
ENDURING WORDS

IN STONE

FROM OUR NATION'S MONUMENTS

BY RYAN COONERTY
PHOTOGRAPHED BY CAROL M. HIGHSMITH

FOREWORD BY DOUGLAS BRINKLEY

 NATIONAL GEOGRAPHIC

WASHINGTON, D.C.

Workers etching the carnelian granite at the entrance to the Franklin Delano Roosevelt Memorial

TABLE OF CONTENTS

(PAGES 2-3) A terra-cotta frieze depicting Civil War forces wraps around Washington, D.C.'s National Building Museum.

FOREWORD

IN 1872, WHEN THEODORE ROOSEVELT was 14 years old, his parents took him on an excursion up the Nile River from Cairo to see the ancient ruins of Karnak, Thebes, and Luxor. Throughout the odyssey, Roosevelt kept a detailed diary, recording that the Egyptian monuments he encountered were "grand, magnificent and awe-inspiring." To Roosevelt, these shrines inspired "thought which can never be spoken."

Unfortunately, at this time the United States had not done a good job of saving either antiquities sites or of building monuments for the ages, and none of the memorials profiled in *Etched in Stone* existed. Instead, affluent Americans like the Roosevelts had to look to Rome or Athens or Cairo for heritage enlightenment.

Luckily, at this time a group of conscientious Americans began taking matters into their own hands. Veterans groups started erecting memorials to honor stricken comrades in Chickamauga and Antietam and Gettysburg, and by 1895, Congress established

Gettysburg National Military Park. As America and TR rose to world prominence, the nation's attention turned to commemorating the past.

What is most impressive about *Etched in Stone* is to see how creative and elegiac the United States has been in memorializing its heritage. Sometimes—as was the case with the monument to the first women's rights convention in Seneca Falls, New York—the wait for grandeur has taken decades. And although the Lincoln Memorial in Washington, D.C., reminds us that our 16th President was the "Great Emancipator," the Clayton Jackson McGhie Memorial in Duluth, Minnesota, provides a sobering truth: Even a presidential proclamation was not enough to eradicate racism. By unveiling bronze statues of three African Americans hanged by a lynch mob in 1920, though, the community was able to redeem itself. Call it memorial-as-apology.

Many of the images in this book are familiar. But how many readers have ever heard of—let alone seen—the International Peace Garden towers located in North Dakota along the Canadian border, or the Anne Frank Human Rights Memorial in Boise, Idaho?

Which brings us back to Theodore Roosevelt, whose memorial in Washington, D.C. bears the quote: "A man's usefulness depends upon his living up to his ideals in so far as he can." All of the memorials in Etched in Stone live up to our nation's highest ideals. They are lasting tributes to the very best instincts we have as a nation: proper reflection for the vicissitudes of the past.   —*Douglas Brinkley*

A 56-foot-long bas-relief in New York City honors the 343 members of the New York Fire Department who died on September 11, 2001.

FOUR SCORE AND SEVEN YEARS
AGO OUR FATHERS BROUGHT FORTH
ON THIS CONTINENT A NEW NATION
CONCEIVED IN LIBERTY AND DEDICA~
TED TO THE PROPOSITION THAT ALL
MEN ARE CREATED EQUAL ·

NOW WE ARE ENGAGED IN A GREAT
CIVIL WAR TESTING WHETHER THAT
NATION OR ANY NATION SO CON~
CEIVED AND SO DEDICATED CAN LONG
ENDURE · WE ARE MET ON A GREAT
BATTLEFIELD OF THAT WAR · WE HAVE
COME TO DEDICATE A PORTION OF
THAT FIELD AS A FINAL RESTING
PLACE FOR THOSE WHO HERE GAVE
THEIR LIVES THAT THAT NATION
MIGHT LIVE · IT IS ALTOGETHER FIT~
TING AND PROPER THAT WE SHOULD
DO THIS · BUT IN A LARGER SENSE
WE CAN NOT DEDICATE~WE CAN NOT
CONSECRATE~WE CAN NOT HALLOW~
THIS GROUND · THE BRAVE MEN LIV~
ING AND DEAD WHO STRUGGLED HERE
HAVE CONSECRATED IT FAR ABOVE
OUR POOR POWER TO ADD OR DETRACT·
THE WORLD WILL LITTLE NOTE NOR
LONG REMEMBER WHAT WE SAY HERE
BUT IT CAN NEVER FORGET WHAT THEY
DID HERE · IT IS FOR US THE LIVING
RATHER TO BE DEDICATED HERE TO
THE UNFINISHED WORK WHICH THEY
WHO FOUGHT HERE HAVE THUS FAR
SO NOBLY ADVANCED · IT IS RATHER FOR
US TO BE HERE DEDICATED TO THE
GREAT TASK REMAINING BEFORE US~
THAT FROM THESE HONORED DEAD
WE TAKE INCREASED DEVOTION TO
THAT CAUSE FOR WHICH THEY GAVE THE
LAST FULL MEASURE OF DEVOTION~
THAT WE HERE HIGHLY RESOLVE THAT
THESE DEAD SHALL NOT HAVE DIED IN
VAIN~THAT THIS NATION UNDER GOD
SHALL HAVE A NEW BIRTH OF FREEDOM~
AND THAT GOVERNMENT OF THE PEOPLE
BY THE PEOPLE FOR THE PEOPLE SHALL
NOT PERISH FROM THE EARTH ·

INTRODUCTION

THIS BOOK WAS BORN ON THE STEPS of the Lincoln Memorial in Washington, D.C. Catching my breath after a jog under the blossoming cherry trees, I rested halfway up the memorial's steps—the very ones that had served as the platform for Martin Luther King, Jr., when he called on his fellow Americans to share his dream of equality.

Closing my eyes, I could imagine the crowd gathered around the Reflecting Pool listening to Dr. King's distinctive cadence and potent metaphors. I could almost feel the electricity of the moment as thousands gathered, invoking the spirit of the Constitution, listening to King preach from his soul, declaring, "When we let freedom ring, when we let it ring from every village and every hamlet, from every state and every city, we will be able to speed up that day when all of God's children, black men and white men, Jews and Gentiles, Protestants and Catholics, will be able to join hands and sing in the words of the old Negro spiritual, Free at last! Free at last! Thank God Almighty, we are free at last!"

My historical daydream was quickly interrupted by the shouting of schoolkids leaving the half dozen tour buses idling in front of the memorial. Families of tourists argued among themselves as they trudged up the steps on their way to check one more obligatory sight off their tour list. Mundane conversations filled the air: Quarrels about the time and place of the next meal and the importance of such and such a celebrity had replaced the oratory that invoked righteousness and self-evident truths. My heart sank, and I wondered if public spaces such as the Lincoln Memorial, a temple to democracy, had somehow lost their ability to inspire, to be relevant.

Disillusioned, I wove my way up the steps through the boisterous crowd. As I walked into the shade of the memorial, Lincoln's enormous statue rose in front of me, serenely seated, resolutely observing the Washington Monument and the Capitol on the

(OPPOSITE) The words of the Gettysburg Address at the Lincoln Memorial have proved timeless.

horizon. A small crowd gathered around the statue, lighting his beard with the flash of their cameras. The larger crowd, however, was grouped to the left, silently reading Lincoln's Gettysburg Address, engraved in a narrow portal on the memorial's southern wall. Young and old alike mouthed:

Four score and seven years ago our fathers brought forth on this continent, a new nation, conceived in Liberty, and dedicated to the proposition that all men are created equal.

They pointed up to the words, slowly moving their fingers from left to right to keep their place.

Now we are engaged in a great civil war, testing whether that nation, or any nation so conceived and so dedicated, can long endure. We are met on a great battle-field of that war. We have come to dedicate a portion of that field, as a final resting place for those who here gave their lives that that nation might live. It is altogether fitting and proper that we should do this.

Parents kneeled next to their children so that in whispers they could explain the difficult words to them.

But, in a larger sense, we can not dedicate—we can not consecrate—we can not hallow—this ground. The brave men, living and dead, who struggled here, have consecrated it, far above our poor power to add or detract. The world will little note nor long remember what we say here, but it can never forget what they did here. It is for us the living, rather, to be dedicated here to the unfinished work which they who fought here have thus far so nobly advanced.

Finally, as they got to the text engraved just above eye level, they moved closer to the wall. The familiar conclusion of Lincoln's address and the stirring ideas set forth seemed to energize them.

It is rather for us to be here dedicated to the great task remaining before us—that from these honored dead we take increased devotion to that cause for which they gave the last full measure of devotion—that we here highly resolve that these dead shall not have died in vain—that this nation, under God, shall have a new birth of freedom—and that government of the people, by the people, for the people shall not perish from the earth.

Visitors finished reading and slipped away as new readers arrived. I stood there reading and rereading the speech with them, feeling them engage with words spoken generations ago. They read the words carved deep into the walls carefully, because they knew that each carefully cut letter was part of the permanent passing of an inspired hope for future generations. They read because the words endure.

Across the United States, on county courthouses and national monuments, below statues and over doorways, are words etched in stone. These poems and quotations are lasting testimonies to what our nation was, is, or aspires to be. Even as the nation and its people succeed and fail in these aspirations, the words in stone remain.

This book is meant to celebrate the displayed words that define our nation. From Emma Lazarus's stiirring "Give me your tired, your poor, / Your huddled masses yearning to breathe free" at the base of the Statue of Liberty, to the motto "Equal Justice Under Law" engraved on the pedimemt above the entrance to the Supreme Court, to prayers for peace on the walls of the International Peace Garden Church in Williston, North Dakota, the sites that were chosen for this book are a concrete manifestation of the values of the country.

In focusing on sites that are tied to historic events and national goals, I was by necessity selective in choosing what to include. There are many engraved words in town squares and on university buildings that are poetic and deeply meaningful to the members of those communities. Someday I hope that a documentation of these sites will be written to provide a more textured view of the American landscape. Because of limited space, the sites in this book were chosen to be geographically and historically diverse, to tell the story of America through time from coast to coast. These are also public spaces—designed as spots for people to enjoy communally.

The words included in this book are not always triumphant. Some—such as those engraved by Chinese immigrants at the detention facility on Angel Island and the words found in the memorials commemorating the Holocaust—remind the reader of both a particular tragedy and of the moments when we, as a nation, failed to live up to our promise. The mission of these sites is to educate the visitor in the hope of preventing tragedies such as these from recurring.

These words found here do not provide a complete and accurate history of the events that inspired them—they were inscribed by committees with the agendas of their time. Nevertheless, they serve a vital function for a country that prizes the future over history and action over contemplation. These words engraved into stone— metaphorically, if not always literally—require that we stand with one another in a public space to remember, mourn, celebrate, dream, and continue to hope, knowing that our children and their children will do the same.   —*Ryan Coonerty, Santa Cruz, 2006*

IN PRAISE OF

PUBLIC LIVES

Robert F. Kennedy addresses an enthusiastic crowd during his campaign for the U.S. Senate in 1964.

IN PRAISE OF PUBLIC LIVES

(OPPOSITE) *Granite entrance pillars at the John F. Kennedy Memorial Park in Cambridge, Massachusetts, contain excerpts from speeches given by the President.*

FROM THE PLAZAS OF EUROPE AND SOUTH AMERICA to the pyramids of Egypt, societies have long built monuments to their leaders. The United States, a relatively young country, did not begin building national monuments until the early 19th century, in part to honor revered leaders, and in part to create national emblems around which the newly formed country could form an identity.

The architectural approaches taken to honor America's giants—Presidents, activists, authors, and thinkers—reflect the prevailing ideals and tastes of the time. Some, like the George Washington Masonic National Memorial, are built to imposing heights, whereas other, more recently constructed memorials, such as the Franklin Delano Roosevelt and Albert Einstein memorials, are at a human scale. The Lincoln Memorial serves as a focal point for the nation's capital, while less than a mile away, the monument to Theodore Roosevelt sits isolated on a forested island. In the end, however, each of these places, in a uniquely American way, has become more about the ideals of those memorialized than the leader memorialized.

Inscribed on the walls of the memorials are not the achievements of these greats of history but rather their hopes and convictions. Dates and facts are relegated to adjacent museums and the speeches of tour guides. The words etched into the walls of the Lincoln and Jefferson memorials tell the visitor little about the Presidencies of the men but much about their views of democracy and governance. The memorials to the Roosevelts are not defined by dates of wars fought and offices won; rather, the Presidents' aspirations are carved deep into stone to provide inspiration for future generations. The words engraved to honor the lives and untimely deaths of the Kennedy brothers are not about the tragedy of loss, but instead communicate the men's hope for humankind. Einstein's inscription is not a mathematical equation; it is his observation on "Joy and amazement of the beauty and grandeur of this world of which man can just form a faint notion."

Most sites, following the American creed, center on action—the future, not the past. The Clemens Center in Elmira, New York, and the memorial to Martin Luther King, Jr., at Morehouse College, exist as living memorials, adding another dimension to the cultural and educational experience of those leaving the theater or the classroom.

Fittingly, the island monument to Theodore Roosevelt, who advocated the creation of national parks, sits at the confluence of several trails that allow visitors to explore protected wilderness.

Some of the memorials, such as those to Franklin D. Roosevelt and Robert F. Kennedy, forsake the wishes of the men themselves to be buried simply; rather, their friends, families, and admirers decided it necessary for future generations to read their timeless speeches about peace and justice.

Nowhere is this application of history to address the issues of modern life more apparent than at the Lincoln Memorial, which has become a shrine to equality rather than to just one man. Civil rights leaders used it as a literal and metaphorical backdrop in their claims for equal rights, and it was the site of a historic concert by African-American opera singer Marian Anderson, barred from singing at a Washington, D.C., concert hall because of her race.

The sites represented in this chapter are a reflection of their time rather than of the population as a whole. But public architecture, like the country, is changing, and is increasingly celebrating and honoring the movements that demanded equality and rights regardless of gender or race.

...We face a moral crisis as a country and a people...The heart of the question is whether all Americans are to be afforded equal rights and equal opportunities, whether we are going to treat our fellow Americans as we want to be treated.

-John F. Kennedy
Report to the American
People on Civil Rights
June 11, 1963

The words of the leaders, in Lincoln's immortal prose, call on "the better angels of our nature." The places may praise public lives, but words engraved deep into their walls celebrate immortal ideals.

GEORGE WASHINGTON MASONIC NATIONAL MEMORIAL

Alexandria, Virginia, 1932

GEORGE WASHINGTON'S FACE has been immortalized on a large scale on Mount Rushmore and on a small scale on U.S. currency, and both the city and state of Washington were named after the soldier turned President. One of the more unusual tributes, though, was constructed in 1932: the George Washington Masonic National Memorial. The Masons—a fraternal order derived from medieval guilds of stone-masons—built the memorial to honor the most famous Mason in history. To lay the cornerstone, President Calvin Coolidge used the same Masonic trowel that Washington wielded to set the cornerstone of the United States Capitol building in 1793.

Inside, a museum showcases historical documents and artifacts from Washington's life; outside, a large stone wall bears an excerpt from a letter Washington wrote in 1786 to James Madison, who represented Virginia in the Continental Congress and who would lead the Constitutional Convention the following year. The words voice Washington's desire for national politics free of factions and selfishness: "Let prejudices and local interests yield to reason. Let us look to our National character, and to things beyond the present period."

(OPPOSITE) Standing 333 feet high, the George Washington Masonic National Memorial commands sweeping views of Virginia, Maryland, and the District of Columbia.

(BELOW) The bronze bas-relief of Washington surmounting his words was first commissioned as part of America's Bicentennial observance and commemorates the 50th anniversary of the memorial

LET PREJUDICES AND LOCAL INTERESTS YIELD TO REASON. LET US LOOK TO OUR NATIONAL CHARACTER AND TO THINGS BEYOND THE PRESENT PERIOD.

Thomas Jefferson Memorial

Washington, D.C., 1943

THE THOMAS JEFFERSON MEMORIAL IN WASHINGTON, D.C., honors a man who, besides being the third President of the United States, was one of the foremost lawyers, architects, statesmen, naturalists, philosophers, and inventors of his—or any—time.

Brilliant as well as insatiably curious, at age 33 Thomas Jefferson drafted the Declaration of Independence in 1776 as part of the original 13 Colonies' quest for independence from England. In so doing he defined the characteristics that became the hallmarks of the new nation. The evocative words of the declaration's preamble, beginning "When in the course of human events, it becomes necessary for one people to dissolve the political bands which have connected them with another," appear on the west wall of the memorial.

At the core of Jefferson's philosophy was a vision of freedom. In 1779, as a member of the Virginia House of Delegates appointed to revise Virginia's laws, he drafted the Statute for Religious Freedom to create "a wall of separation between church and state." Its language, mixed with Jefferson's explanation to James Madison, also decorates the wall of the statue chamber: "Almighty God hath created the mind free. ... All attempts to influence it by temporal punishments or burthens ... are a departure from the plan of the Holy Author of our religion. ... No man shall be compelled to frequent or support any religious worship or ministry or shall otherwise suffer on account of his religious opinions or belief ..."

Jefferson considered one of his greatest accomplishments to be the founding of the University of Virginia, and at his request, his epitaph lauds his role as the university's "father" and omits his tenure as President of the United States. Jefferson fostered the belief that universities were necessary to democratize the nation, and the campus and curriculum he designed have become models for public universities around the country. His passion is reflected in the quotations engraved on the memorial's eastern wall: "Establish the law for educating the common people. This it is the business of the state to effect and on a general plan."

The memorial's placement threatened the Tidal Basin's storied cherry trees, and its Roman design was criticized as competing with the Lincoln Memorial's. But President Franklin D. Roosevelt's last-minute intervention resolved the situation, and the memorial was dedicated on the 200th anniversary of Jefferson's birth.

I HAVE SWORN UPON THE ALTAR OF GOD
ETERNAL HOSTILITY AGAINST EVERY FORM
OF TYRANNY OVER THE MIND OF MAN.

—THOMAS JEFFERSON, *rotunda dome*

LINCOLN MEMORIAL

Washington, D.C., 1922

THE LINCOLN MEMORIAL serves as the spiritual and architectural anchor of Washington, D.C. The memorial, a Greek temple inhabited only by the imposing statue of a 19th-century American and his legendary words, defies the ephemeral. In the nation's capital, it is hallowed ground.

During his term of office, from 1860 to 1865, the 16th President witnessed the division of his country by a civil war in which almost one million Americans would die. Abraham Lincoln's leadership was essential in maintaining the Union, and his words, such as the Emancipation Proclamation, which set in motion the freeing of four million slaves, defined the moral code for the country's future. But on April 14, 1865, only days after the war ended, the 56-year-old Lincoln was shot; he died the following day. Two years later Congress created the Lincoln Monument Association to pay homage to the prematurely fallen President; it would be some 50 years before a memorial was realized, with construction starting in 1917.

The memorial sits at the western end of the National Mall, the 200-foot-long Reflecting Pool at its base stretching to the Washington Monument, with the U.S. Capitol beyond. Thirty-six marble columns, the only ornaments to the memorial's square right angles, represent the number of states in the Union when Lincoln died. Above the columns a frieze features bas-relief sculptures of the 48 states in the Union at the memorial's completion. The temple design is not accidental: Lincoln's speeches have become part of American fundamental civic theology. The words of Lincoln's Second Inaugural Address give voice to the nation's identity as unified and just, but it is his 1863 Gettysburg Address, engraved on the memorial's south wall beneath a mural depicting an angel freeing a slave, that articulates the relevance of Lincoln's life, memory, and words. Lincoln claimed his words would be forgotten by history, yet they make the memorial a conscience for the nation across time and place for future generations.

(OPPOSITE) Daniel Chester French's marble statue of 16th President Abraham Lincoln gazes solemnly toward the Mall in Washington, D.C.

IN THIS TEMPLE

AS IN THE HEARTS

OF THE PEOPLE FOR WHOM

HE SAVED THE UNION

THE MEMORY

OF ABRAHAM LINCOLN

IS ENSHRINED FOREVER.

—Words etched above the statue of Abraham Lincoln

FONDLY DO WE HOPE, FERVENTLY DO WE PRAY,
THAT THIS MIGHTY SCOURGE OF WAR MAY SPEEDILY PASS AWAY.

—ABRAHAM LINCOLN, *Second Inaugural Address, north wall*

CLEMENS CENTER

Elmira, New, York, 1977

Praising the work of Samuel Clemens—whose pen name, Mark Twain, came from his experiences as a riverboat captain—author Ernest Hemingway wrote: "All modern American literature comes from one book by Mark Twain called 'Huckleberry Finn.' There was nothing before. And there has been nothing as good since." Clemens's books serve as a social critique of race relations in the country, studies of the American character, and wondrously funny and moving stories of imagination and youth.

For more than 20 years, Clemens escaped to Quarry Farm outside of Elmira, New York, to spend his summers conjuring stories such as *The Adventures of Huckleberry Finn, The Adventures of Tom Sawyer,* and *A Connecticut Yankee in King Arthur's Court*, tales that would entertain generations and form the foundation of modern American literature.

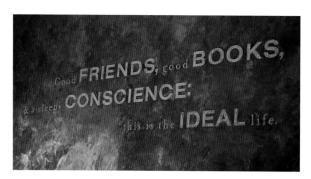

Samuel Clemens's tongue-in-cheek words adorn the lobby wall of the center named in his honor.

In Elmira, Clemens found friendship, love, and the quiet necessary to write. While in Elmira he awoke early and would spend several hours writing before wandering into town to meet friends, buy cigars, play billiards, and regale the locals with stories of his adventures in the American West and beyond. Clemens and his family are buried in Elmira's idyllic Woodlawn Cemetery.

Clemens's memory lives on in Elmira through festivals, tours, and the Clemens Center in downtown Elmira. The center was built 15 years after Clemens's death in 1925 but was not renamed in his honor until 1977. Designed to showcase vaudeville acts and silent films, it quickly gained a reputation as a premier regional theater between New York City and Buffalo. After a flood damaged the theater in 1972, the Elmira community raised funds to save it from demolition. Renaming the center for Elmira's most famous summer resident, the theater chose to engrave quotations from the writings of Mark Twain.

In an exuberant mix of capital and lowercase letters, the colorful quotations swirl on the lobby and mezzanine walls, as well as the center's lounge and exterior facade, giving the building humor and life.

The Mark Twain study at Quarry Farm, now on the campus of Elmira College, was the birthplace of many of Clemens's classic tales.

MANHOOD

"A MAN'S USEFULNESS
DEPENDS UPON HIS LIVING UP TO
HIS IDEALS
IN SO FAR AS HE CAN

IT IS HARD TO FAIL ● BUT IT IS WORSE
NEVER TO HAVE TRIED TO SUCCEED

ALL DARING & COURAGE
ALL IRON ENDURANCE OF MISFORTUNE

MAKE FOR A FINER & NOBLER TYPE OF
❀ MANHOOD ❀

THEODORE ROOSEVELT MEMORIAL

Washington, D.C., 1967

THEODORE ROOSEVELT ISLAND, an oasis of green adjacent to a bustling city, provides a fitting location to honor a man whose life and legacy were shaped by open spaces. The memorial, in the island's center, comprises fountains, a 17-foot statue of the 26th President, and four etched tablets whose themes encapsulate the values of one of this country's most popular leaders.

Despite suffering from a number of childhood diseases, Theodore Roosevelt (1858-1919) became an ardent naturalist, athlete, world traveler, and soldier, as well as an author, civil service reformer, head of the New York City police, governor of New York, and Vice President of the United States, all by the age of 42. He achieved national fame in 1898 when he resigned as secretary of the Navy to organize the Rough Riders in the Spanish-American War. This sense of duty is reflected on the tablet entitled STATE, engraved with such quotations as: "If I must choose between righteousness and peace, I choose righteousness."

Although born in New York City, Roosevelt later found solace living on a ranch in the Dakota Territory following the sudden deaths of his wife and his mother in 1884. His profound dedication to nature is clear on the stone bearing that name: "The nation behaves well if it treats the natural resources as assets which it must turn over to the next generation increased and not impaired in value." These words, from a 1910 speech Roosevelt gave in Kansas outlining his political philosophy of a New Nationalism, were reflected in his establishment of five national parks in the early 1900s and of the National Forest Service and the first federal game preserve in 1905.

The tablet MANHOOD highlights Roosevelt's philosophy of a life well lived, touting maxims such as: "Only those are fit to live who do not fear to die; and none are fit to die who have shrunk from the joy of life and the duty of life."

Roosevelt's legacy is one of committed public service, courageous adventures in service to his country, and a never ending sense of curiosity. These traits form the final theme. On the tablet YOUTH, Roosevelt's admonitions refer not to a period of life, but rather to its spirit: "I want to see you game, boys, I want to see you brave and manly, and I also want to see you gentle and tender," he told students at Friends School in Washington, D.C., in 1907.

(OPPOSITE) A detail from MANHOOD, one of four 21-foot granite tablets etched with the words of 26th President Theodore Roosevelt

THERE IS DELIGHT
IN THE HARDY LIFE
OF THE OPEN.

—THEODORE ROOSEVELT,
Nature panel

*A stone bridge leads to
the Theodore Roosevelt
Memorial on wooded
Theodore Roosevelt
Island. It is a fitting
site for the man who, in
1905, established the
National Forest Service.*

FRANKLIN DELANO ROOSEVELT MEMORIAL

Washington, D.C., 1997

THE DESIGN OF THE MEMORIAL honoring Franklin Delano Roosevelt, the first 20th-century President to be memorialized on the National Mall, takes a more human and interactive approach than that of other presidential monuments. A self-contained park, which incorporates the adjacent Tidal Basin and landscape into its design, the memorial invites visitors to walk—literally—through Roosevelt's Presidency.

Franklin Delano Roosevelt (1882-1945) served as President of the United States during the most difficult of times. When he was first elected in 1932, the country was in the depths of an economic depression. Nearly every bank in the country had failed, and millions of Americans were out of work. Roosevelt promised the country a "New Deal" and enacted dozens of government programs to spur the economy, increase employment, and create an economic safety net. Many of his administration's programs, such as Social Security, still exist.

Early in Roosevelt's third term, the United States entered World War II, and the President had to mobilize the country for war both in Europe and in the Pacific. He created a "Grand Alliance" of countries through the United Nations to combat Nazi Germany and Japan. Although he died in office in 1945, on the eve of an armistice, Roosevelt is credited with providing the leadership that allowed the United States to win World War II.

Throughout Roosevelt's Presidency, Eleanor Roosevelt served as the political eyes and ears for her husband, whose ability to travel grew limited after he contracted polio in 1921. She visited the administration's New Deal relief projects so that she could report back her observations, but also became an advocate in her own right for the poor and for minorities. After President Roosevelt's death, she continued an active public life. President Harry S. Truman appointed her to the U.S. Delegation to the United Nations General Assembly, a position she held until 1953. She later served as chairwoman of the Human Rights Commission of the United Nations during the drafting of the Universal Declaration of Human Rights.

In 1955 Congress established a commission to build a monument to President Roosevelt, but it was 1974 before the commission selected as designer Lawrence Halprin, a world-renowned landscape architect known for integrating architecture with the environment.

'THEY (WHO) SEEK TO ESTABLISH
SYSTEMS OF GOVERNMENT BASED ON
THE REGIMENTATION OF ALL HUMAN
BEINGS BY A HANDFUL OF INDIVIDUAL
RULERS... CALL THIS A NEW ORDER.
IT IS NOT NEW AND IT IS NOT ORDER.

President Roosevelt's Scottish terrier Fala poses with his master beneath an excerpt from a speech to White House correspondents.

FREEDOM OF SPEECH

FREEDOM OF WORSHIP

FREEDOM FROM WANT

FREEDOM FROM FEAR

—FRANKLIN DELANO ROOSEVELT,
Address to Congress, the memorial's fourth area

An aerial view of Lawrence Halprin's study model for the memorial highlights the effect of water.

Reviewing Roosevelt's Presidency, Halprin decided that "no one object, building, or statue could express the broad scope of those years. No single image could capture the multiplicity of events, challenges, difficulties and successes."

The memorial is organized thematically by Roosevelt's presidential terms, and key statements by Franklin and Eleanor Roosevelt are carved at eye level, creating intimacy. Roosevelt was a gifted speaker; his words rang with authority and resolution, offering the American people hope. The first area concentrates on Roosevelt's optimism and the importance of the first hundred days of his Presidency, including the engraved words of his Inaugural Address, which assured the country that "the only thing we have to fear is fear itself."

(BELOW) *Franklin Roosevelt stands on a campaign train with the help of his son James in 1934.*

Visitors then move through to the President's second term, focusing on how the Roosevelt Administration dealt with the Great Depression and unemployment. Roosevelt's 1933 proposal to Congress to create a Civilian Conservation Corps, extolling the "moral and spiritual value of such work," is engraved into stone and surrounded by sculptures depicting the struggles faced by out-of-work Americans.

The final two areas of the memorial center on the work the President and First Lady did on behalf of a lasting peace. The President's abhorrence of war is highlighted on a granite wall: "I have seen war. I have seen war on land and sea. I have seen blood running from the wounded ... I have seen the dead in the mud. I have seen cities destroyed ... I have seen children starving. I have seen the agony of mothers and wives. I hate war." These words, delivered in 1936 during the Spanish Civil War, were inspired by Roosevelt's tour of the battlefields in France as assistant secretary of the Navy during World War I.

The memorial closes with calls for peace and justice. Engraved next to a statue of Eleanor Roosevelt is her husband's statement to Congress in his report on the Crimea (Yalta) Conference of February 1945, near the close of World War II: "The structure of world peace cannot be the work of one man, or one party, or one nation. It must be a peace which rests on the cooperative effort of the whole world."

(FOLLOWING PAGES) *Sculptures of a rural couple and men in a bread line complement the words taken from Roosevelt's Second Inaugural Address.*

Martin Luther King's tomb in Atlanta bears the words: "Free at last. Free at last. Thank God Almighty I'm Free at last."

It must be borne in mind that the tragedy in life

doesn't lie in not reaching your goal.

The tragedy lies in having no goal to reach.

—BENJAMIN MAYS, *wall of quotations in Martin Luther King Jr. International Chapel*

Some men see things as they are and ask, "Why?"

I dream things that never were and ask, "Why not?"

—Edward Kennedy, *quoting George Bernard Shaw in a eulogy to his brother*

ROBERT F. KENNEDY MEMORIAL

Arlington, Virginia, 1968

ON A HILLSIDE IN ARLINGTON NATIONAL CEMETERY, overlooking the grand marble monuments of Washington, D.C., a small white cross marks the grave of Robert F. Kennedy. It reflects Kennedy's wish to be buried without extravagance.

Kennedy's early years were spent in the shadow of his father, businessman and diplomat Joseph P. Kennedy, and war hero brothers Joseph and John Kennedy. But as a U.S. Senator he called attention to poverty and injustice in America—particularly in the Mississippi Delta and inner cities and against Native Americans and migrant farmworkers. And on June 4, 1968, after a campaign that sought to unite middle-class people with the poor and dispossessed, he won the California Democratic presidential primary. That night an assassin shot him.

Opposite Kennedy's grave marker is a small plaza designed in 1971 by architect I. M. Pei at the request of the Kennedy family. Excerpts from two of Kennedy's most notable speeches are engraved on two low walls. One is from a speech he gave in 1966 to college students in apartheid South Africa: "It is from numberless diverse acts of courage ... that ... human history is shaped. Each time a man stands up for an ideal, or acts to improve the lot of others, or strikes out against injustice, he sends forth a tiny ripple of hope, and crossing each other from a million different centers of energy and daring, those ripples build a current that can sweep down the mightiest walls of oppression and resistance."

An adjacent stone carries part of a five-minute impromptu speech to a predominantly African-American crowd in Indianapolis, Indiana, the night Martin Luther King, Jr., was assassinated. Kennedy first informed the crowd of King's death, then attempted to both soothe their grief and call for compassion in a difficult time: "Aeschylus ... wrote: 'Even in our sleep, pain which cannot forget falls drop by drop upon the heart, until, in our own despair, against our will, comes wisdom through the awful grace of God.' What we need in the United States is not division; what we need in the United States is not hatred; what we need in the United States is not violence and lawlessness; but is love and wisdom, and compassion toward one another, and a feeling of justice toward those who still suffer within our country, whether they be white or whether they be black."

(OPPOSITE) Kennedy children visit Robert Kennedy's grave in 1971, the year a memorial plaza was added to the site.

IT IS FROM
NUMBERLESS
DIVERSE ACTS
OF COURAGE…
THAT…
HUMAN HISTORY
IS SHAPED.

— ROBERT KENNEDY,
*excerpt from a 1966 speech
given at the University of
Cape Town, South Africa,
memorial plaza wall*

*Simply carved
and engraved, the
gravestones of
Arlington National
Cemetery eloquently
honor America's
fallen servicemen
and women.*

ORDINARY

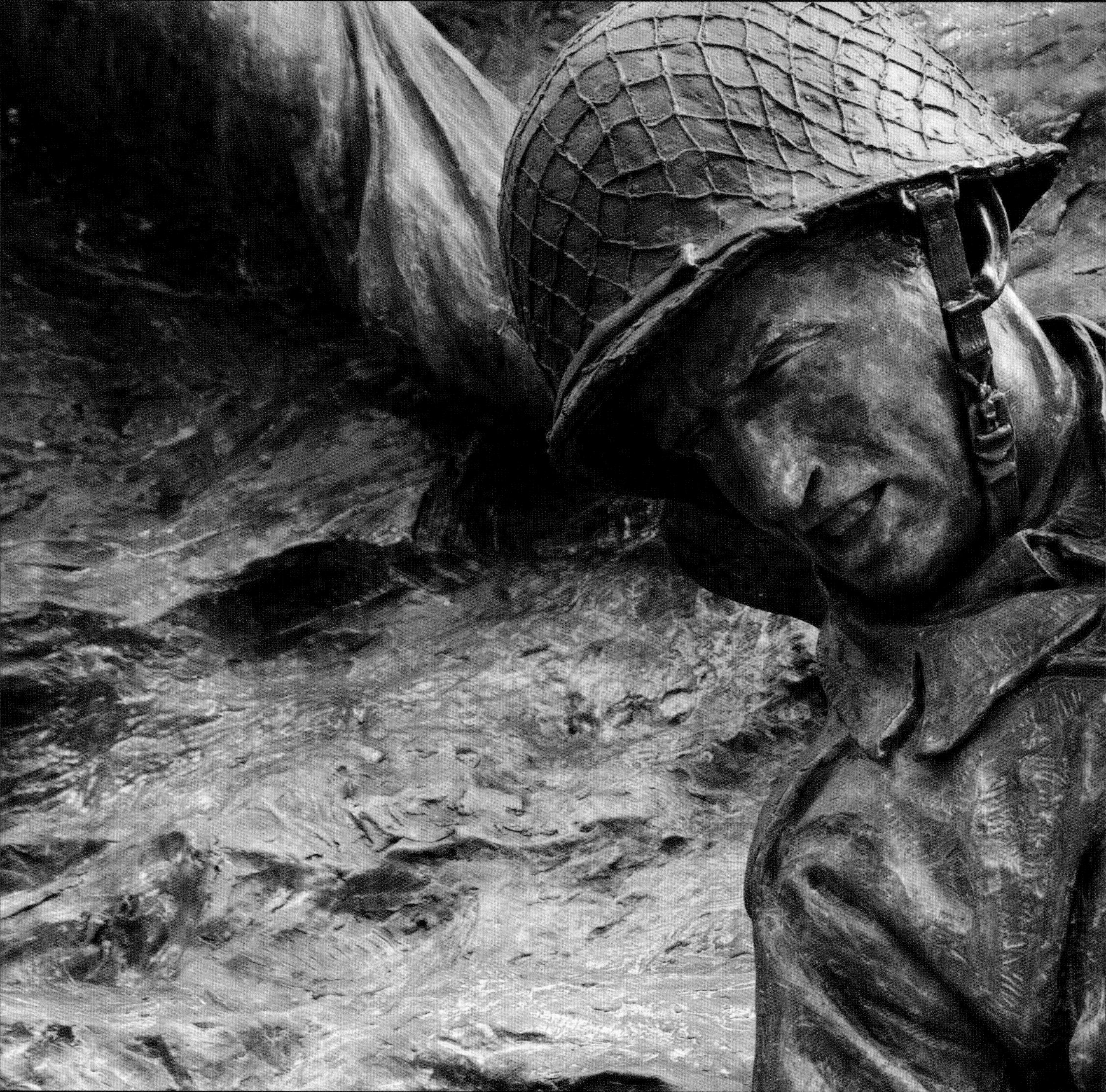

HEROES

Ordinary Heroes

N<small>O MATTER HOW GREAT THE LEADER,</small> history demands the heroic acts of the many. Wars are not won and lost with speeches and strategy; battles are decided with bravery and blood by soldiers in the trenches. Justice necessitates more than a law in a book; it also needs the neighborhood police officer walking the beat.

Too often, this reality is missing in national public spaces. The military general is memorialized with a bronze statue in the town square, the President with a park or airport, while the people who contributed their labor and lives in service to the campaigns of these leaders are relegated to the memories of family or the anonymity of time.

Under heavy machine-gun fire American soldiers land on the Normandy beaches of France on June 6, 1944.

The sites in this chapter center on the many men and women who followed orders and led by action—those who knew that they would not be remembered in history books, but—over a day, month, year or lifetime—put themselves in harm's way because the larger forces of history required it.

This chapter begins with the petroglyphs in the Utah desert where Native American tribes left a pictorial history in a sandstone bluff. The centuries-old etchings exist because their inscribers wanted future passersby to know that there were forefathers and -mothers who lived, struggled, and found comfort in the same shade of a mesa.

The bulk of the chapter focuses on the memorials honoring the fallen soldiers of America's wars—from the two minutemen who fell in Concord, thus launching the Revolutionary War's "shot heard round the world," to the thousands of troops who read the letter from Gen. Dwight Eisenhower on the eve of D-Day in World War II reminding them that "The eyes of the world are upon you. The hopes and prayers of liberty-loving people everywhere march with you." These sites put the individual's role in the arc of history.

The words etched on war memorials illuminate the politics and preferences of the time. The Civil War memorial to Robert Gould Shaw and the African-American 54th Regiment uses the romantic poetry of the era, while the newly constructed World War II Memorial employs awe-inspiring speeches to provide the context for the sacrifice of hundreds of thousands of soldiers.

In counterpoint is the most visited and discussed war memorial—Maya Lin's Vietnam Veterans Memorial. The V-shaped wall of 58,249 engraved names of soldiers lost in the Vietnam conflict eschews the larger political interpretation for the focus on the individual sacrifice. It forsakes the poetry that romanticizes the battlefield for the simple black stone that forces visitors to see their reflection amid the names evoking the awful consequences of war.

The simplicity of the words on memorials honoring fallen police officers and firefighters conveys the code of honor implicit in these jobs. "The Alarm Rang and We Answered" and "In Valor There is Hope" are timeless in their description of jobs that have changed dramatically over time but will always require sacrifice for the greater good.

Regardless of historical event, the etched words of this chapter exist because ordinary citizens in extraordinary times embodied the observation by Admiral Nimitz engraved on the Marine Corp Memorial: "Uncommon Valor was a Common Virtue."

NEWSPAPER ROCK STATE HISTORIC MONUMENT

Southeastern Utah

R ESTING IN THE SHADE OF A MESA rising out of the Utah desert, a sandstone promontory near a small river lined with cottonwood trees offers proof that the desire to leave a lasting impression of one's life on Earth transcends time and culture. For more than 2,000 years neighboring tribes and visitors have drawn illustrations on Newspaper Rock and other rocks and caves in the state, creating what a writer in the pages of NATIONAL GEOGRAPHIC magazine called a "wilderness Louvre."

Newspaper Rock, which the Navajo call Tse' Hane (rock that tells a story), contains hundreds of petroglyphs—images or symbols used in lieu of an alphabet—carved into the rock surface. They are thought to have been inscribed by the Ute, Fremont, Anasazi, and Navajo peoples as they farmed the valley, centuries before the arrival of Spanish explorers and American settlers. Some of the extraordinary images include representations of animals, footprints, and hunters shooting their prey. The artist, or recorders, carved deep into the dark coating of fine-grained clay minerals, exposing the golden underlying rock. As a result, the petroglyphs remain as defined and bright as when first carved

The oldest petroglyphs discovered in the world thus far are estimated to be more than 12,000 years old. Petroglyphs—derived from the Greek words *petros*, meaning "stone," and *glyphein*, meaning "to carve"—have been found in Europe, Africa, Asia, Australia, and North and South America. The images appear to resemble one another in theme and style despite the separation of time and place. Researchers have not been able to explain the markings, but the general consensus is that they have religious and cultural meanings.

Thousands of petroglyph sites exist in the American Southwest, from California to Texas and up through Colorado. Efforts to preserve and study these treasured locations are gaining momentum. Newspaper Rock was initially managed by Utah State Parks, placed on the National Register of Historic Places in 1974, and in 1993 turned over to the Bureau of Land Management. Today a growing number of people travel the main road into the Needles District of Canyonlands National Park to look at the petroglyphs, curious about a place where symbols compete with centuries of weather and geology to convey their message in stone.

The still bright petroglyphs of Utah's Newspaper Rock remain undeciphered.

HERE ONCE THE EMBATTLED
FARMERS STOOD
AND FIRED THE SHOT
HEARD ROUND THE WORLD

—RALPH WALDO EMERSON,
from "Concord Hymn," base of the statue

MINUTE MAN NATIONAL HISTORIC STATE PARK

Concord, Massachusetts, 1875

WITH ONE FOOT IN FRONT OF THE OTHER, rifle forward, shirtsleeves up, his plow and jacket left behind, the Minute Man personifies the American ideal of action and patriotism. In the spring of 1775 tensions were rising in the American Colonies. For more than a decade Americans had chafed at British rule, and on April 19, British soldiers marched from Boston to the township of Concord to destroy American munitions and close the Massachusetts Assembly, which was instigating anti-British resistance.

The first skirmish occurred in Lexington, where professional British soldiers exchanged shots with an American militia composed of farmers and craftspeople, who earned the title minutemen for being able to organize and fight on short notice. As the British marched from Lexington to Concord, the minutemen, although outnumbered, outtrained, and underarmed, used their knowledge of the area to fire at the troops from behind trees and buildings.

When the British reached the Old North Bridge in Concord, where the Minute Man statue stands today, the Concord militia confronted the British Army, believing that the village was about to be razed. The British fired and two Americans were killed. The militia fought back, killing 270 British troops while driving the army back to Boston. The American Revolution had begun. By war's end a generation of ordinary men, fighting for their rights and independence, succeeded in defeating the world's most powerful empire.

On the centennial of the battle in Concord, a citizens committee was formed to construct a memorial to the event. The committee chose local sculptor Daniel Chester French to craft a monument to the farmer-soldiers who rose against the British redcoats on that spring afternoon in 1775. French, eventually earning recognition as one of the finest sculptors of his generation, would later fashion the Lincoln Memorial. Fellow Concord resident Ralph Waldo Emerson, one of the committee's members, offered to write a poem in honor of the men. Rendered in gold lettering on the Minute Man's pedestal, Emerson's "Concord Hymn" speaks to the importance of the skirmish, which few of its participants could have dreamed of.

(OPPOSITE) Daniel Chester French's bronze statue depicts a farmer abandoning his plow to take up arms in the Revolutionary War.

(FOLLOWING PAGES) An obelisk commemorating the first armed conflict of the Revolution stands before Concord's Old North Bridge, with the Minute Man statue visible in the background.

By the rude bridge
that arched the flood,
Their flag to April's
breeze unfurled.

—Ralph Waldo Emerson,
from "Concord Hymn," base of the statue

Robert Gould Shaw and 54th Regiment Memorial

Boston, Massachusetts, 1897

(ABOVE) A member of the 54th Regiment marches in a detail of Augustus Saint-Gaudens's bronze relief sculpture.

(OPPOSITE) Col. Robert Gould Shaw, shown on horseback, fell during the attack on Fort Wagner.

THE ROBERT GOULD SHAW AND 54TH REGIMENT MEMORIAL on the northeast corner of Boston Common honors the pivotal role a small group of ordinary men played in maintaining the unity of the United States.

In 1861, with the country engaged in civil war, the Massachusetts governor recruited a regiment of black freemen to fight for the Union. A 25-year-old white colonel and native Bostonian, Robert Gould Shaw, volunteered to command the 600 men, who volunteered for the suicidal assault on Fort Wagner in South Carolina. On July 18, 1863, the regiment charged the sandy slope of the fortress. The Confederate Army opened fire. Within hours, Shaw was killed and more than 200 of his men were killed, missing, or taken prisoner.

In 1865 Joshua B. Smith—a former fugitive slave and employee of the Shaw household and a state representative from Cambridge, Massachusetts—established a memorial fund. Augustus Saint-Gaudens created an 11-foot-by-14-foot relief sculpture depicting Shaw on horseback amid his troops, their faces detailed and resolute. A verse from poet James Russell Lowell honors his friend Shaw. Harvard University President Charles Eliot, whose words are inscribed on the back, said the soldiers of the 54th were "brave in action patient under heavy and dangerous labors and cheerful amid hardships and privations."

RIGHT IN THE VAN,

   ON THE RED RAMPART'S SLIPPERY SWELL,

WITH HEART THAT BEAT A CHARGE, HE FELL

FOEWARD, AS FITS A MAN;

   BUT THE HIGH SOUL BURNS ON TO LIGHT MEN'S FEET

WHERE DEATH FOR NOBLE ENDS MAKES DYING SWEET.

— JAMES RUSSELL LOWELL, *front of the memorial*

GETTYSBURG NATIONAL MILITARY PARK

Gettysburg, Pennsylvania, 1895

THE FORESTS, FIELDS, AND ROLLING HILLS of Gettysburg Battlefield are all the more powerful today for their tranquility. On early weekday mornings, a visitor can cross in solitude an area once filled with the horrors of war but now populated with the silence of nature and hundreds of stone memorials. More than 1,300 monuments, markers, and memorials stand on the fields of Gettysburg. Some are simple, some ornate. All offer testimony to the tragedy and valor of war.

In July 1863 a bloody battle for the soul of a nation took place on the farmlands of Pennsylvania. Confederate Gen. Robert E. Lee, in an ambitious attempt to win a decisive victory in the North, faced the Union Army of Gen. George Gordon Meade. At the end of

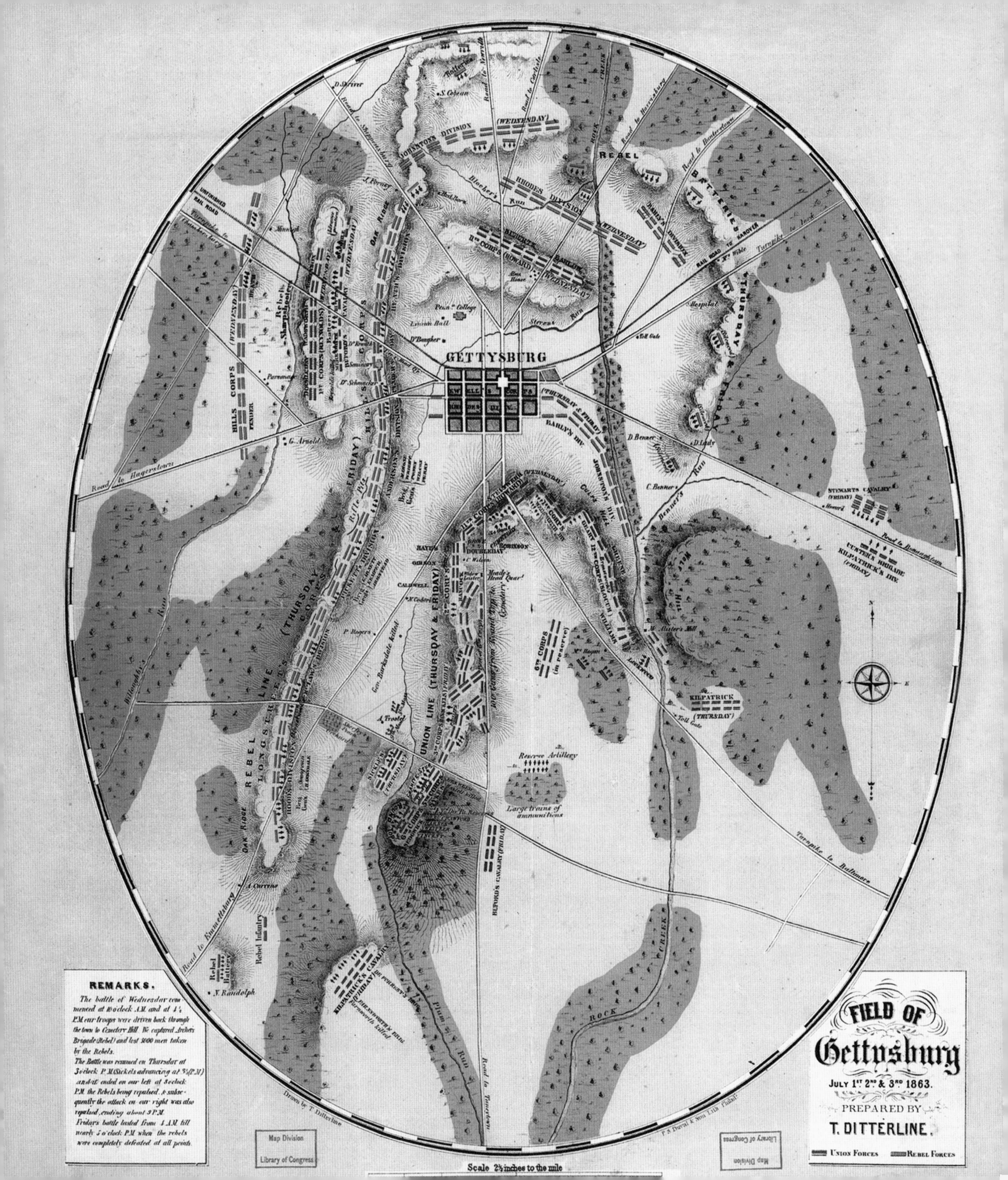

FIELD OF
Gettysburg
JULY 1ST 2ND & 3RD 1863.
PREPARED BY
T. DITTERLINE.
UNION FORCES
REBEL FORCES
Scale 2½ inches to the mile
REMARKS.
The battle of Wednesday commenced at 10 o'clock A.M. and at 4½ P.M. our troops were driven back through the town to Cemetery Hill. We captured Archer's Brigade (Rebel) and lost 5000 men taken by the Rebels.
The Battle was resumed on Thursday at 3 o'clock P.M. Sickels advancing at 3½ (P.M.) and at ended on our left at 8 o'clock P.M. the Rebels being repulsed, & subsequently the attack on our right was also repulsed, ending about 9 P.M.
Friday's battle lasted from 4 A.M. till nearly 5 o'clock P.M. when the rebels were completely defeated at all points.
GETTYSBURG
Drawn by T. Ditterline
P. S. Duval & Son Lith. Philad.
Map Division
Library of Congress
JOHNSTON'S DIVISION
(WEDNESDAY)
RHODES DIVISION
(WEDNESDAY)
REBEL
BATTERIES
EARLY'S DIVISION
11TH CORPS (HOWARD)
BARLOW
(WEDNESDAY)
THURSDAY & FRIDAY
HILLS CORPS
(WEDNESDAY)
HILL'S CORPS
1ST CORPS (REYNOLDS)
REBEL LINE
LONGSTREET'S CORPS (THURSDAY)
UNION LINE (THURSDAY & FRIDAY)
6TH CORPS (in reserve)
STEWART'S CAVALRY (FRIDAY)
CUSTER'S BRIGADE
KILPATRICK'S DIV
(FRIDAY)
KILPATRICK
(THURSDAY)
BUFORD'S CAVALRY (FRIDAY)
KILPATRICK'S CAVALRY (FRIDAY)
Reserve Artillery
Large trains of ammunitions
Meade's Head Quar.
Penn. College
Lutheran Hall
Seminary
Oak Ridge
Oak Hill
Cemetery Hill
Culp's Hill
Wolf Hill
Rock Creek
Plum Run
Willoughby Run
Marsh Run
Benner's Run
Stevens Run
Rock Creek
Road to Harrisburg
Road to Carlisle
Road to Mummasburg
Road to Hunterstown
Rail Road to Hanover
Turnpike to York
Road to Bonaughtown
Turnpike to Baltimore
Road to Taneytown
Road to Emmettsburg
Road to Hagerstown
Turnpike to Chambersburg
Unfinished Rail Road
Rebel Sharpshooters
Rebel Infantry
Rebel Battery
Gen. Barksdale killed
Toll Gate
Hospital
N. Randolph
A. Currens
G. Arnold
P. Rogers
A. Trostel
D. Benner
C. Benner
D. Lady
McAlister's Mill

NOW WE ARE ENGAGED IN
A GREAT CIVIL WAR,
TESTING WHETHER THAT
NATION, OR ANY NATION SO
CONCEIVED AND SO DEDICATED
CAN LONG ENDURE.

—ABRAHAM LINCOLN, *Gettysburg Address*

the three days of fighting, Lee was forced to retreat; the Civil War fortunes of the North had turned, and the blood of 51,000 American casualties soaked the earth.

While local communities struggled to treat the wounded and recover from the devastation, local attorney David McConaughy bought parcels of land where prominent battles had occurred, with the hope of creating a memorial park. Soon other locals joined his cause, and by April 1864, while the Civil War still raged, the state chartered the Gettysburg Battlefield Memorial Association.

Little was done, however, and the battlefield was left largely untouched until the late 1870s, when veterans groups began placing memorials to commemorate fallen comrades. Reinvigorated, the Memorial Association encouraged the honoring of the dead: By the 25th anniversary of the battle, nearly 200 memorials had been dedicated. Two years later another 150 monuments were added.

In 1895 Congress established Gettysburg National Military Park; 522 acres and the Memorial Association were moved under the control of the War Department. Because of the battlefield's location in the North, only two monuments had been erected to honor fallen

soldiers of the Confederacy. The War Department's commission on Gettysburg worked tirelessly to expand the park and increase the number of monuments for both Union and Confederate units.

Statues, bronze reliefs, simple markers, and elaborate monuments—the memorials vary widely. Most are of stone, and etched with the names of the company, regiment, or division that fought during the battle's three bloody days; they are set approximately where the combat took place. One of the simplest and most touching is the monument to the Minnesota First Infantry. Adjacent to a statue of a soldier charging into battle a marker simply states: "Minnesota 52 Bodies." Some of the larger memorials are more flowery: "We sleep here in obedience to law; when duty called we came, when country called, we died," reads the Georgia Monument, and "Your Names Are Inscribed on Fame's Immortal Scroll" is engraved on the base of the Alabama Monument. The Sharp Shooters of Andrew, Massachusetts, memorial wryly says, "In God We Put Our Trust, But Kept Our Powder Dry."

On the 75th anniversary of the Battle of Gettysburg, President Franklin Roosevelt brought together 1,800 Civil War veterans from both the Union and the Confederacy to dedicate a memorial to "Peace Eternal in a Nation United" on Oak Hill, overlooking the July 1, 1863, battlefield. Inscribed beneath an eternal flame are the words "An Enduring Light to Guide in Unity and Fellowship."

(BELOW) Sculptor Caspar Buberl's terra-cotta frieze of Union soldiers at Gettysburg wraps around Washington, D.C.'s National Building Museum, the former Pension Building serving Civil War veterans.

(FOLLOWING PAGES) Gettysburg Cemetery serves as a resting place for veterans of the nation's major wars and conflicts.

REST ON, EMBALMED AND SAINTED DEAD,

DEAR AS THE BLOOD YE GAVE,

NO IMPIOUS FOOTSTEP HERE SHALL TREAD

THE HERBAGE OF YOUR GRAVE.

NOR SHALL YOUR GLORY BE FORGOT

WHILE FAME HER RECORD KEEPS,

FOR HONOR POINTS THE HALLOWED SPOT

WHERE VALOR PROUDLY SLEEPS.

—THEODORE O'HARA, *"The Bivouac of the Dead,"*
placed throughout the grounds

NATIONAL D-DAY MEMORIAL

Bedford, Virginia, 2001

(OPPOSITE) Evoking the invasion, bronze soldiers crawl and wade on the concrete and in the fountains of the National D-Day Memorial.

BEDFORD, VIRGINIA, IS IN MANY WAYS a typical small American town . However, only a few generations ago this community sacrificed more than most one June morning in a conflict an ocean away.

In 1941 three dozen Bedford men enlisted to fight in World War II. Many were assigned to the 29th Infantry Division, and although they did not know it, they would be part of one of the most daring and deadly military maneuvers in history: On June 6, 1944, the 29th Infantry participated in the D-Day invasion. As the invading forces stormed the beaches of Normandy, they met with ammunition, mortars, land mines, and harrowing cliffs. The Allies prevailed, however, and within months the foothold gained at Normandy proved to be a turning point of the war: Allied troops soon marched into a liberated Paris and eventually to Berlin.

But victory came at a terrible price. An estimated 14,000 troops were killed in the months preparing for D-Day; another 10,000 Allied soldiers were killed or wounded on D-Day itself, including 2,000 American deaths on Omaha Beach. Among those casualties were 21 Bedford men, 19 of them in the first 15 minutes of the invasion. Bedford, with a population then of only 3,200, proportionally suffered more losses than any other community. In recognition of this sacrifice, Congress chose the town to be the site of the National D-Day Memorial.

The memorial offers an arresting sight: nine acres of statues of soldiers crawling, wading, and dying on its concrete and in its fountains. The centerpiece is a large vertical relief that depicts soldiers struggling to crawl up the hillsides of Omaha Beach beneath a 44-and-a-half-foot arch inscribed with the mission's name: "Overlord." An adjacent wall carries, beneath the patch of the Supreme Headquarters of the Allied Expeditionary Force, Gen. Dwight David Eisenhower's order, given to every soldier on the day of the invasion. In it he assured his men: "In company with our brave Allies and brothers-in-arms on other Fronts you will bring about the destruction of the German war machine, the elimination of Nazi tyranny over the oppressed peoples of Europe, and security for ourselves in a free world."

66

SOLDIERS, SAILORS AND AIRMEN OF THE ALLIED EXPEDITIONARY FORCE:
YOU ARE ABOUT TO EMBARK UPON THE GREAT CRUSADE, TOWARD WHICH
WE HAVE STRIVEN THESE MANY MONTHS. THE EYES OF THE WORLD
ARE UPON YOU. THE HOPES AND PRAYERS OF LIBERTY-LOVING PEOPLE
EVERYWHERE MARCH WITH YOU…

— GEN. DWIGHT D. EISNHOWER,
D-Day order, engraved on a wall of the memorial

WORLD WAR II MEMORIAL

Washington, D.C., 2004

THE WORLD WAR II MEMORIAL, a sea of nearly blinding white granite in the nation's capital, seems to shout simultaneously the expansive themes of triumph, patriotism, and sacrifice. The tablet at the memorial's entrance recognizes the intensity of this place and provides its historical and geographic context: "Here in the presence of Washington and Lincoln, one the eighteenth century father, and the other the nineteenth century preserver of our nation, we honor those twentieth century Americans who took up the struggle during the Second World War and made the sacrifices to perpetuate the gift our forefathers entrusted to us: a nation conceived in liberty and justice."

This statement and the memorial's design and placement are a conscious effort to recognize World War II as a defining moment in American history. "This National World War II Memorial," wrote historian Douglas Brinkley, "is meant to pay homage to an entire generation. ... It honors not just the young G.I. storming ashore at Normandy or the admiral deciding how to best win the Battle of Midway, but the American people as a whole. The memorial salutes the tireless women who worked in the textile mills to make parachutes and the world-class engineers who designed essential new parts for the B-24 bomber. It is, at its essence, a glorious memorial that pays homage to Franklin D. Roosevelt's Four Freedoms, a national shrine for the enduring triumph of Jeffersonian-Hamiltonian Democracy."

World War II was a global struggle, although it began in 1939 as a European war. By its conclusion in 1945, 61 countries and three-quarters of the world's population had been involved. Fifty-five million people died. Battles occurred on three continents, and the total cost of the war is estimated to be one trillion dollars. It was the deadliest, most expensive war in human history. For the United States, the war took place in two theaters—the Atlantic against Nazi Germany and its allies, and the Pacific against Japan. To fight a global war on two fronts, the United

(BELOW) An excerpt from President Franklin Roosevelt's request to Congress for a declaration of war is etched into a wall in the memorial plaza.

(OPPOSITE) Fountains dance in the memorial's Rainbow Pool in front of the Atlantic Theater pavilion.

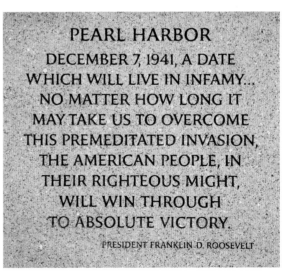

PEARL HARBOR
DECEMBER 7, 1941, A DATE
WHICH WILL LIVE IN INFAMY...
NO MATTER HOW LONG IT
MAY TAKE US TO OVERCOME
THIS PREMEDITATED INVASION,
THE AMERICAN PEOPLE, IN
THEIR RIGHTEOUS MIGHT,
WILL WIN THROUGH
TO ABSOLUTE VICTORY.

PRESIDENT FRANKLIN D. ROOSEVELT

MARINE CORPS WAR MEMORIAL

Washington, D.C., 1995

(BELOW) *Photographer Joe Rosenthal's iconic World War II photograph was the inspiration for the tribute to the U.S. Marine Corps.*

(OPPOSITE) *Six 32-foot bronze soldiers on the Marine Corps War Memorial struggle day and night to raise the American flag.*

THE MARINE CORPS WAR MEMORIAL is modeled on one of the most iconic war photographs ever taken. Photographer Joe Rosenthal captured the scene on February 23, 1945, after one of World War II's bloodiest battles. Two days earlier, Marines had launched an assault on the small Pacific island of Iwo Jima, facing more than 640 embedded gun nests and pillboxes. After two days of fighting, a 40-man division fought their way up Mount Suribachi, a dormant volcano at the southern tip of the island, and raised a small American flag. That afternoon, four Marines returned to place a larger flag in the crater. As they struggled to pierce the rocky ground with a makeshift flagpole, two other soldiers joined the effort and Rosenthal photographed the men.

The cost of taking Iwo Jima proved high, with 17,372 Marines wounded and 5,931 killed. Three of the men photographed raising the flag that day were killed within the month. But the memorial, sculpted by Felix W. de Weldon, a World War II veteran moved by Rosenthal's photograph, is dedicated not only to those killed on Iwo Jima but to all the Marines who have died in defense of the United States. Using the physical attributes of each of the men on Mount Suribachi that day, he began a precise effort to re-create the moment in bronze. The casting process took nearly three years, and three trucks were needed to move the monument. It is the largest bronze sculpture in the world.

The memorial commands an impressive view of Washington, D.C., and the Potomac River. The memorial statue's granite base is engraved with the names and dates of every major Marine Corps engagement since the Corps's founding in 1775.

UNCOMMON VALOR WAS A COMMON VIRTUE

— ADM. CHESTER NIMITZ, *memorial base*

OUR NATION HONORS HER SONS AND DAUGHTERS

WHO ANSWERED THE CALL

TO DEFEND A COUNTRY THEY NEVER KNEW

AND A PEOPLE THEY NEVER MET.

— Engraving at the Korean War Veterans Memorial's Field of Service

KOREAN WAR VETERANS MEMORIAL

Washington, D.C., 1995

THE KOREAN WAR VETERANS MEMORIAL does not focus on individuals lost, as the Vietnam Memorial does, or celebrate victory in the grand manner of the World War II Memorial. Rather, in words and symbols, it conveys a message of sacrifice and of historical complexity.

The Korean War began in 1950 as a conflict between North and South Korea over their common boundary. Until an armistice was reached in 1953, it became a struggle between global superpowers and political ideologies that led to the deaths of some four million people. Hundreds of thousands of U.S. military personnel served; 54,246 died, and 103,284 were wounded. In addition, 628,833 U.N. personnel died and more than one million were wounded. However, the legacy of the Korean War was lost between the celebration of World War II and the debate over the Vietnam War.

After the Vietnam Veterans Memorial was placed on the National Mall in 1982, a public effort got under way to recognize the veterans of the Korean War. Congress authorized the American Battle Monuments Commission to create a memorial, and President Ronald Reagan appointed an advisory board. The commission eventually chose a design that portrays a squad on patrol. World War II veteran and artist Frank Gaylord sculpted the 19 soldiers. A 143-foot wall of black granite runs on the soldiers' left side, its highly polished surface reflecting the men and creating the impression of 38 soldiers walking in formation. It symbolizes their efforts to push North Korean troops back to the 38th parallel, the border agreed upon by the U.S. and the Soviet Union at the conclusion of World War II. The stainless-steel soldiers represent each of the four branches of the military and are multiethnic to acknowledge that the Korean War was the first time that the military had consciously sought to integrate troops.

Artist Louis Nelson sandblasted intricate images, taken from original photographs, to honor those who had served, both in battle and in support. On an adjacent stone wall are engraved the names of the 22 countries that supported the United Nations' efforts. However, it is the short statement etched into the stone that serves as both a tribute to the soldiers and a blunt statement about sacrifice: Freedom Is Not Free.

(OPPOSITE) A detail from one of the brushed stainless-steel statues at the Korean War Veterans Memorial

FREEDOM
IS NOT FREE.

— *Engraving at the memorial's
Pool of Remembrance*

*Nineteen ground
troops of varying
ranks, branches
of service, and
ethnicities advance
in winter gear.*

VIETNAM VETERANS MEMORIAL

Washington, D.C. 1982

IN 1982, MAYA LIN, the daughter of Chinese immigrants, wrote a description of a "rift in the earth"—her vision for a memorial to soldiers lost in a divisive and deadly war. These sentences described what is arguably the world's most visited, discussed, and thought-provoking memorial. It is intimate, historic, and artistic. It is an austere design for a complicated war.

Approximately 3.2 million Vietnamese were killed in the two-decade-long war between Communist-ruled North Vietnam and anti-Communist South Vietnam following the withdrawal of France as colonial ruler in 1954. Another 1.5 million to 2 million Laotians and Cambodians were killed or displaced. The United States entered the conflict in 1965, and by 1969 more than half a million U.S. troops were stationed in Vietnam; more than 58,000 lost their lives.

Although the Vietnam War caused a fissure in the United States, in the late 1970s a movement to honor those Americans who had died in Vietnam began. Congress authorized the creation of a memorial, and a private group, led by Vietnam veteran Jan Scruggs, raised funds. Lin, a 21-year-old Yale student, was selected from the more than 1,400 applicants who entered a national design competition, yet her design, forsaking the traditional elements of a war memorial, was immediately controversial. Following congressional hearings on the appropriateness of the design, a traditional statue of soldiers was added. (A statue commemorating women's service was added later.)

In 1982, less than a decade after the end of the war, the memorial—familiarly known as the Wall—was dedicated. Veterans and families of those lost gathered around it searching for a father's, brother's, or friend's name. In her book *Boundaries*, Lin says that casualties are listed by year, because if visitors find one name, "chances are you will see the others close by, and you will see yourself reflected through them."

The Wall, designed as a creased book, is both intimate and public. The number of names, etched in capital letters, is overwhelming. Inevitably, upon finding a familiar name, people will gently touch the wall—connecting themselves to a memory. Some leave flowers, flags, or notes, which are collected each day and stored by the Smithsonian Institution.

THIS MEMORIAL IS FOR THOSE WHO HAVE DIED,

AND FOR US TO REMEMBER THEM.

—MAYA YING LIN, *designer,*
Vietnam Veterans Memorial

DEWVEALL • ROBERTO DOMINGUEZ • JOHN J FOGARTY III • RALPH E GE
ER • AMIL JACKSON Jr • RALPH E JOHNSON • STEVE E JORDAN • STEVEN T
NANDO L LOZANO • JAMES A LUCKEY • JOSEPH L MEADE • RONALD D MEL
E MYERS • ANDERSON D BOLTON • CLIFFORD L NEWBERRY • BRUCE D O
ULYSSES G QUEENER Jr • DAVID W RIEMER • JAMES P RIGGINS • JAY DEE RUM
ANK D SMITHERMAN • JERRY W TALLEY • ROGER L VICKERS • JON F WARMBR
PH A AGUIRRE • LORAN L BERGER • MARTIN J GIMBERT • SHERMAN D BRADF
ENRY R BROADTMAN Jr • MARVIN COOK Jr • DONALD B DEAN • DAVID P DO
RUSSELL L EQUI • WILLARD J EVANS • JOHN A BOYLE • JORGE L GUZMAN-PA
Y HENSLEY • GARY D HUMPHRIES • DOUGLAS D JANSSEN • KENNETH P JOHN
ON • IVAN W JONES • LAWRENCE L KEISTER • MARIO M LAGUNA • ALAN K LAN
GARY W MAY • JOHN F MEYER • MICHAEL R MICHELS • WILLIAM R MOHRHA
AM R NEVILLE • STANLEY H NEWMAN • CHARLES H WATKINS Jr • RODNEY W PA
DAVID C RUSH • MICHAEL J SCHICKEL • LYLE W SCHROEDER • DANIEL E SINGLE
Y • DAVID W STERLING • BRADLEY E SUCHKA • DENNIS E ULSTAD • STANLEY F U
JERRY LEE O'NEAL • BRUCE R WELGE • ROGER C BEALL • RAYMOND F BEAUCH
RICHARD CLARK • JOHN E CONGER Jr • WALLACE T CO
J DEVINE • WALTER L F

WALLACE C BERGSTROM Jr · DWAIN L BIBEY · GERALD R CA

· GARY J COYLE · PATRICK E McCULLOUGH · ROBERT M DAVENP

· STANLEY D FARRO · RICHARD B GARRETT · ALFRED A C

PETER C HURLOCK · PAUL R JARVIS · GAYLAND E

CHRISTOPHER MITCHELL · MICHAEL L MITCHELL · RUSSELL E MOKE

· CHARLES H OXENDINE · STANLEY PATTERSON · JAMES E PIERC

RODNEY G SHANK · JAMES R SMITH · LARRY STEVENSON

· JAMES L WARD · GARY N YOUNG · LONNIE BRIDGES

· THOMAS E CLARK · ROBERT D DE BOARD · WARD C EVANS · F

· DAVID B GRAHAM · DAVID P HAEGELE · LAWRENCE C HAWLEY · CHR

LLOYD J HUCKS · NATHANIEL IRVING · PERRY D JOHN

· VICTOR R LANDES · ROBERT O MAYHEW · JAMES B McKN

ROBERT H PARCHER Jr · ALEXANDER A S PEOPLES · THEUS J POUND

· ALVIN L SHADWICK · JAMES M SKOMSKI · RICHARD L SKOU

JOSEPH O STRICKLAND · MANUEL GURROLA ULLOA · CALVIN W WILKIN

· JOHNNIE W ATOR · STEVEN R BAUER · DOUGLAS J BEVERIDGE

· BENITO CONCHOL

· LYMAN R

· ROBERT L HET

"The Lone Sailor" stands vigil in the United States Navy Memorial's granite amphitheater.

UNITED STATES NAVY MEMORIAL

Washington, D.C., 1987

In 1791 GEORGE WASHINGTON appointed Pierre L'Enfant to design the "federal city" of Washington, D.C., for the new government. In addition to envisioning a large park in the middle of the city (now the National Mall) and the placement of the White House and Congress, L'Enfant proposed a monument to "consecrate" the Navy's "progress and achievements." L'Enfant's vision for the capital took more than a hundred years to implement, but his desire for a monument to the Navy required almost twice as long to complete.

A private foundation was formed in 1977 to construct a memorial to those who serve in the branch of service that has taken part in every major conflict and played a decisive role in the Civil War, the Spanish-American War, and the World Wars. The memorial's broad mission, cast into a granite compass rose, is "In honor of those who served to form the heritage of the United States Navy / In tribute to those who perished to provide peace and security for our maritime nation / In gratitude to those now serving."

The memorial is centered by a hundred-foot granite relief map (next page) of the world, which forms an outdoor amphitheater where military bands perform regularly. To properly score the tiles to reflect the division between sea and land, new stonecutting technology had to be developed, making this the only map of its kind in the world. Surrounding the map are four pools of light-blue water. Fountains lift the water into the air, and when there is a breeze, cause a mist to sprinkle visitors, creating the sensation of being at sea. At the dedication of the memorial, water collected by submarines from the seven seas was poured into the fountains. Memorable phrases from naval history are carved into the stone walls of the memorial, such as John Paul Jones's pronouncement "I have not yet begun to fight!" during the Revolutionary War, and Adm. David Farragut's defiant Civil War order "Damn the torpedoes, full steam ahead." The words to the first verse of the "Navy Hymn," a nearly 150-year-old hymn that is sung to honor those lost at sea, are engraved along the memorial's steps, a sobering reminder of the dangers faced by those called to service.

ETERNAL FATHER,
STRONG TO SAVE,
WHOSE ARM HATH
BOUND THE
RESTLESS WAVE,
WHO BID'ST
THE MIGHTY
OCEAN DEEP
ITS OWN APPOINTED
LIMITS KEEP;
O HEAR US WHEN WE
CRY TO THEE,
FOR THOSE IN PERIL
ON THE SEA.

— "NAVY HYMN," *memorial steps*

(FOLLOWING PAGES)
Pedestrians cast
deep shadows on
the memorial's
one-of-a-kind map.

Don't give up the ship.

—Capt. James Lawrence, *memorial wall*

The Memorial Wall at the Fire Museum of Memphis is dedicated to firefighters who have lost their lives serving the Memphis community.

FIRE MUSEUM OF MEMPHIS

Memphis, Tennessee, 1998

STANDING IN FRONT OF THE BRIGHT RED FIREHOUSE DOORS of the Memphis Fire Museum on a sweltering summer night it is not difficult to imagine the place alive with action. From 1910 until the mid-1960s, the firefighters of the station on Adams Street in downtown Memphis were first on the scene for emergencies big and small, and for more than 250 years, firefighters in the United States have engaged in the same ritual—rushing from safety to danger at the sounding of the bell. The Fire Museum of Memphis was built to honor those who respond to that alarm.

Housed in a restored turn-of-the-century fire station that could no longer be used, the museum offers visitors the opportunity to learn about fire safety and the life of the firefighter. Outside the firehouse's doors is a large Memorial Wall dedicated to firefighters who have lost their lives since 1880 serving the Memphis community.

The memorial, funded by the local firefighters union, is a sculpted relief of five larger-than-life firefighters emerging from the rubble of a fire. One is injured and being carried by his comrades, while another, head in hands, sits exhausted from his efforts.

> THE ALARM RANG
> AND WE ANSWERED
>
> —*Memorial Wall*

Today, there are more than one million firefighters in the United States, more than three-quarters of whom are volunteers. These firefighters, career and volunteer, will respond to more than 1.5 million reported fires in a given year, and in the process an average of more than 150 will die and thousands will be injured.

In Memphis, every year local firefighters and those from around the world gather at the Memorial Wall to celebrate the heroism of those who die in the line of duty. It is a place where they can find comfort and meaning. "The Wall is a powerful symbol for us. It is the place we gather when we lose a firefighter ... to be there for each other," noted Memphis Division Chief Henry A. Posey, a 29-year veteran of the Fire Department.

In the end, the Fire Museum's Memorial Wall is a reminder to those who visit the museum, or even just catch a glimpse of the wall as they pass by, of the daily sacrifice of firefighters for their community. As author Kurt Vonnegut once wrote, "I can think of no more stirring symbol of man's humanity to man than a fire engine."

NATIONAL LAW ENFORCEMENT OFFICERS MEMORIAL

Washington, D.C., 1991

EVERY DAY MORE THAN HALF A MILLION POLICE OFFICERS report for duty in the United States, and, on average, one officer is killed every 53 hours. The names of more than 17,500 police officers killed in the line of duty engraved on the Walls of Remembrance at the National Law Enforcement Memorial offer a vivid reminder of the sometimes dangerous intersection of law and justice.

Located on three acres in Judiciary Square, an open space surrounded by courthouses, the memorial centers on a reflecting pool, set among tree-lined pathways and gardens.

The engraved names stretch across centuries: Deputy Sheriff Isaac Smith of New York City, killed on May 17, 1792, is the first officer known to die in the line of duty. Anna Hart, a prison matron in Ohio, killed in 1916, is the first female officer honored. Family, friends, and fellow officers often leave notes, flowers, and memorabilia beneath the names of their loved ones and colleagues.

The memorial's inscribed quotations are succinctly descriptive of the meaning of service and sacrifice. One wall, with a bronze lion intently standing guard above, is engraved, "It Is Not How These Officers Died That Made Them Heroes. It Is How They Lived."

IN VALOR

THERE IS HOPE

—TACITUS, *wall adjacent to memorial*

(RIGHT) The memorial logo is embedded in a central plaza.

(OPPOSITE) Life-size bronze lions symbolically guard the names of the fallen.

MAY

WITNESS

WE NEVER FORGET.
TOWER LADDER

A bronze memorial, on a firehouse across from where the World Trade Center's South Tower once stood, honors the firefighters who died on September 11.

Bearing Witness

The sites profiled in this chapter—memorializing the worst injustices and tragedies in the nation's history—attempt the nearly impossible task of providing meaning for acts that were often meaningless. By their nature these spaces must be a place for the living and the dead, a place of reconciliation for justice delayed and justice denied—a public space for private grief. These sites must be relevant when those who knew the victims have long since passed and their lives and loss are assigned to a few words inscribed on a wall, a bench, or a pedestal.

James E. Young, in his book *The Texture of Memory*, notes the difficult nature of building such memorials. He cites Alex Krieger, a child of Holocaust survivors and one of the organizers of the New England Holocaust Memorial project: "It is not for my parents

that I pursue this endeavor. ... This memorial will be for me. Because I was not there, and did not suffer, I cannot remember. Therefore, I very much need to be reminded. This memorial will be for my six-month-old daughter, who will need to be reminded even more. It will be for her children, who will need to be reminded still more. We must build such a memorial for all the generations who, by distance from the actual events and people, will depend on it to activate [memory]."

The subjects of the memorials in this chapter cut across time and subject, but themes emerge. The chapter begins with the Salem witchcraft hysteria of colonial America. Although the trials took place three centuries ago, similar scapegoating and persecution of people based on fear and social instability continued into the 20th century with the internment of Japanese Americans during World War II and the blacklisting of Communists during the Cold War.

These shameful subjects have only recently been memorialized, because they question the nation's commitment to its stated ideals. It is often easier to forget than to remember and to explain.

This was the experience of the Slavery Memorial in Savannah, Georgia, and the Clayton Jackson McGhie Memorial in Duluth, Minnesota. In Savannah, citizens raised concerns about highlighting the horrific institution of slavery in a tourist area that once served as a slave auction site. Similarly, the placement of a memorial delineating a lynching in downtown Duluth required the citizenry to come to terms with the event. In both cases the communities have healed, and, it is hoped, the lessons of tragedy are being applied to combat injustice today.

One of the more remarkable sites in this chapter is the Angel Island immigration facility. Unlike the other sites, this one was created by the victims: Chinese immigrants detained in terrible conditions carved a poetry of despair into the barracks walls, commemorating their time there. They etched their own history, leaving future generations a firsthand account of their pain.

The more recent tragedies of the Oklahoma City bombing and the September 11 attacks are just beginning to be formed in public spaces. The memorials will struggle to give meaning to the ever present grief of family and friends for decades to come. Over time, the memorials will change, becoming a historical device—a place to provide context, facts, and meaning about singular events to future generations.

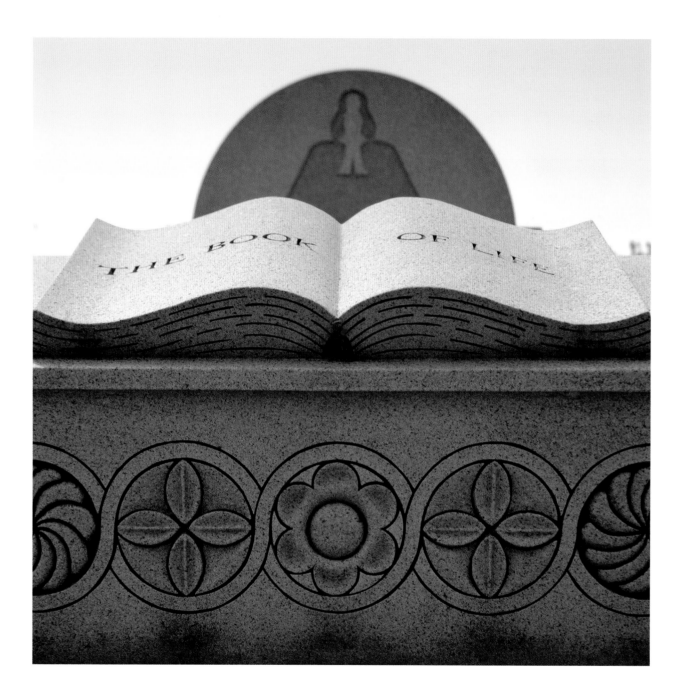

AMEN. AMEN. A FALSE TONGUE WILL NEVER MAKE A GUILTY PERSON.

— SUZANNA MARTIN, *witchcraft trial victim, memorial tablet*

SALEM VILLAGE WITCHCRAFT VICTIMS' MEMORIAL

Danvers, Massachusetts, 1992

SEVENTEEN MILES NORTH OF BOSTON sits a town with a deep New England history. First recognized as Salem Village in 1672, the city of Danvers was less well known and influential than its neighbor, Salem Town. The village marked its place in history, however, in 1692, when that summer 19 men and women were tried and convicted of witchcraft. All were hanged. Another man was crushed with stones for refusing to submit to a trial, while at least four other people died in prison before their trials began. Hundreds were charged and dozens arrested in a panic based on fear, jealousies, and community strife. All the victims proclaimed their innocence in the face of charges from their neighbors and fellow parishioners. The exact cause of the panic is still unknown.

The Salem Village Witchcraft Victims' Memorial was built by the community of Danvers to honor the memory of those killed in the witchcraft hysteria of 1692. Exactly 300 years after that tragic summer, the memorial—with the names of the victims and their protestations of innocence carved in granite—was dedicated to stand as a "reminder that each generation must confront intolerance and witch hunts with integrity, clear vision and courage."

(BELOW) *A large-scale reproduction of the shackles worn by those accused of witchcraft rests at the base of the Salem witchcraft victims' memorial.*

(OPPOSITE) *The memorial's centerpiece replicates a bible box, commonly used by Puritans to hold important papers.*

SLAVERY MONUMENT

Savannah, Georgia, 2002

(ABOVE) *A character in the television movie* Roots *is shackled by chains like those at the foot of the Slavery Monument's statue.*

(OPPOSITE) *The Slavery Monument stands near where the first slaves came ashore.*

SINCE 1733, SAVANNAH, GEORGIA'S RIVERFRONT has defined the community. Goods were brought to the city to be bought, sold, and traded. Today the port continues to prosper, not only in commerce but also as a historical site and tourist attraction. Monuments, gardens, and historic homes remind visitors of the city's rich past. In 2002 the Savannah community installed a monument on the riverfront to remind people that at one time trade at this port also dealt in human cargo.

In 1991 Abigail Jordan, a Savannah resident and the granddaughter of a slave, was asked by African-American tourists why none of the 43 monuments in the city recognized the contributions of blacks to the community. That question began a decade-long—sometimes contentious—struggle to properly honor the history and contributions of African Americans. Jordan established the African-American Monument Association, and after seven years, won city approval for the erection of a bronze statue depicting a modern-day African-American family with broken chains at their feet. The statue was to be placed on the riverfront where the first slaves were brought to Georgia. Almost immediately, however, the memorial's intended inscription proved to be controversial and delayed the project for several years.

Poet and memoirist Maya Angelou had granted permission for the use of an unpublished quotation of hers: "We were stolen, sold and bought together from the African continent. We got on the slave ships together. We lay back to belly in the holds of the slave ships in each others' excrement and urine together, sometimes died together, and our lifeless bodies thrown overboard together." Savannah City Council members felt that the quote was too graphic. After much debate, eventually Angelou offered to add an uplifting phrase at the end: "Today, we are standing up together, with faith and even some joy."

With the amended language, the city council unanimously approved the monument's design. Jordan donated $100,000 to the project, which represented most of her life's savings. On July 27, 2002, more than 350 years after Georgia had legalized the importation of slaves, the monument recognizing their suffering was dedicated, with Abigail Jordan looking on proudly.

TODAY,

WE ARE STANDING UP

TOGETHER,

WITH FAITH

AND EVEN SOME JOY.

—MAYA ANGELOU,
monument base

ANGEL ISLAND
IMMIGRATION STATION

San Francisco, California, 1983

S URROUNDED BY THE BLUE WATERS OF SAN FRANCISCO BAY, beautiful Angel Island commands spectacular views of San Francisco and the Marin headlands. Due to its size and strategic location, the island has attracted many visitors over the years, giving it a rich cultural history. Three thousand years ago the Miwok tribe hunted and fished the island. Later, it was a refuge for Spanish explorers, served as a cattle ranch, and in 1863 welcomed the establishment of a United States Army post.

Its most notable use was as an immigration station. Opened in 1910, the immigration facilities were built to be an "Ellis Island of the West," with the expectation that thousands of European immigrants would travel the newly constructed Panama Canal to the West Coast. However, the outbreak of World War I changed the makeup of the immigrants seeking to come to the United States. Instead of Europeans, Chinese immigrants were processed through Angel Island. Between its opening and 1940, Angel Island served as the point of entry for approximately 175,000 Chinese immigrants. They came with the same hopes as other immigrants coming to America; however, instead of being welcomed with open arms, the Chinese at Angel Island were met with detainments and grueling interrogations, which lasted months and sometimes even years. Between 11 percent and 30 percent of the prospective immigrants arriving at Angel Island were deported, while the deportation rate on the East Coast was only 1 percent to 2 percent.

The conditions on Angel Island were terrible, the barracks dirty and crowded, and between interrogations the immigrants were locked up 24 hours a day, with very little opportunity to exercise or go outside. The only exceptions to the outright ban on Chinese

(BELOW) The calligraphy with which Angel Island immigrants recorded their despair took many forms over the years.

calligraphy carved into bare redwood

ink brush calligraphy over bare redwood

calligraphy carved into painted walls

successive layers of oil-based paint and more carved calligraphy

final layers of oil-based paint

interior walls of detention barracks

埃 煥 嘗
山 野
山 望
阮 既
阮

(OPPOSITE) A slant of light illuminates the poems carved into the barracks walls.

(LEFT) The Japanese—like these "picture brides" having their passports inspected—were the second largest group to pass through Angel Island.

(OPPOSITE) The dilapidated state of the barracks effectively hid in plain sight the poetry carved into the walls years before.

immigrants, after the Chinese Exclusion Act was passed in 1882, were for merchants, clergy, diplomats, teachers, and students, and the arrival of the necessary "proof" could take months or even years. Documenting their despair, the detainees carved intricate poetry on the walls of their barracks. One of the hundreds of poems written by unknown immigrants reads, "From now on, I am departing far from this building / All of my fellow villagers are rejoicing with me / Don't say that everything within is Western styled / Even if it is built of jade, it has turned into a cage."

The poetry was nearly lost forever. By 1970 the abandoned immigration station had fallen into disrepair and was scheduled for demolition, when state park ranger Alexander Weiss discovered the poetry with the help of a flashlight. A committee was formed to save the station and translate the poetry. After raising public awareness of the station and millions of dollars to begin its restoration, in 1997 Congress designated the station a national historic landmark.

THE DAY I AM RID OF THIS PRISON AND ATTAIN SUCCESS, I MUST REMEMBER THAT THIS CHAPTER ONCE EXISTED.

— AUTHOR UNKOWN, *barracks wall*

CLAYTON JACKSON McGHIE MEMORIAL

Duluth, Minnesota, 2003

(OPPOSITE) *The bronze images of lynching victims Elias Clayton, Elmer Jackson, and Isaac McGhie look out on downtown Duluth, Minnesota.*

AMID THE RESTAURANTS, SHOPS, AND OFFICE BUILDINGS of downtown Duluth, Minnesota, stands a memorial that is striking both for its artistry and for its very existence. The Clayton Jackson McGhie Memorial calls attention to three young men who were lynched by a mob on those downtown streets, and uses the horror of their death to teach future generations about tolerance and compassion.

On the evening of June 15, 1920, Elias Clayton, 19; Elmer Jackson, 22; and Isaac McGhie, 20, were seized by a mob from the Duluth City Jail, where they were wrongly being held as suspects in the raping of a white woman. The mob, estimated to be as many as 10,000 strong, tortured and beat Clayton, Jackson, and McGhie before hanging them from a lamppost in downtown Duluth, a lynching that was photographed and distributed widely on a postcard. Although three men were eventually charged and were convicted of rioting, the longest sentence handed out was two years, and no one was charged with murder.

The story went largely untold for the next 70 years, until journalist Michael Fedo uncovered newspaper accounts of the lynching while researching a historical novel. Consumed with the story of a lynching in his hometown, he wrote what was later titled *The Lynchings in Duluth* in 1979. Slowly the story of that June night in 1920 reemerged into public consciousness, and a community group convinced city officials that it was worth memorializing.

The memorial comprises bronze images of the slain men, and walls engraved with quotations by a variety of authors, such as Martin Luther King, Jr.; poet Rumi; philosopher Bertrand Russell; and playwright George Bernard Shaw. Journalist Anthony Porter Payton chose the quotations, which he says show "the universality of human nature, good and bad."

At the dedication ceremony, the great-grandson of one of the organizers of the mob that killed Clayton, Jackson, and McGhie, not knowing whether his great-grandfather felt remorse, apologized to the victims: "I stand here as a representative of his legacy and I willingly place that responsibility on my shoulders."

AN EVENT HAS HAPPENED UPON WHICH IT IS DIFFICULT TO SPEAK AND IMPOSSIBLE TO REMAIN SILENT.

—EDMUND BURKE, *memorial wall*

A young Japanese-American girl in Hayward, California, waits for the bus that will take her to an internment camp.

Japanese American Historical Plaza

Portland, Oregon, 1990

(ABOVE) *A copper column at the Japanses American Historical Plaza's entrance shows two generations of Issei arriving in America.*

THE 13 BASALT STONES of the Japanese American Historical Plaza in Portland, Oregon's Tom McCall Waterfront Park solemnize the U.S. internment of Japanese Americans during World War II, following Japan's bombing of Pearl Harbor. Each stone is engraved with a brief anonymous poem and the name of an internment camp. But the plaza, a collaboration of landscape designer Robert Murase and poet Lawson Inada—both interned as children—is more than a memorial to the injustice of the internment; it is an account of the Japanese experience in America.

The first stone honors the Issei generation—men and women who immigrated to the United States from Japan: "Mighty Willamette! / Beautiful friend, / I am learning, / I am practicing to say your name." The theme of assimilation continues on the next stone, representing the Nisei, first-generation Americans: "Sure, I go to school / Same as you. / I'm an American."

The next stones speak of the isolation and pain of internment: "Rounded up / In the sweltering yard / Unable to endure any longer / Standing in line / Some collapse." Camps in the barren deserts of the West housed some 110,000 Japanese Americans in harsh conditions: "Black smoke rolls / Across the blue sky. / Winter chills our bones. / This is Mindoka." But even worse than the conditions was the pain that lay in knowing that their loyalty to the country was questioned: "Our young men and women / Joined the Army, too / They are proud to be American." Indeed, a regiment of Japanese Americans volunteered from the camps and fought bravely for their adopted country in Europe.

With the end of the war, the Japanese were released and allowed to return home, but while interned, many had lost their jobs, businesses, and homes. The next generations, the Sansei and Yonsei, had to reconcile and come to terms with their country's actions. The concluding stones recognize this struggle: "Going home, / Feeling cheated, / Gripping my daughter's hand, / I tell her we're leaving / Without emotion." The U.S. government issued a formal apology in 1988 and offered some reparations to affected families. The final stone looks to the future: "With new hope, / We build new lives. / Why complain when it rains? / This is what it means to be free."

WITH NEW HOPE,
WE BUILD NEW LIVES.
WHY COMPLAIN WHEN
IT RAINS?
THIS IS WHAT IT MEANS
TO BE FREE.

— ANONYMOUS,
final stone of the memorial

Shadows dance
across a carved
inscription on a
stone in the Japanese
American
Historical Plaza.

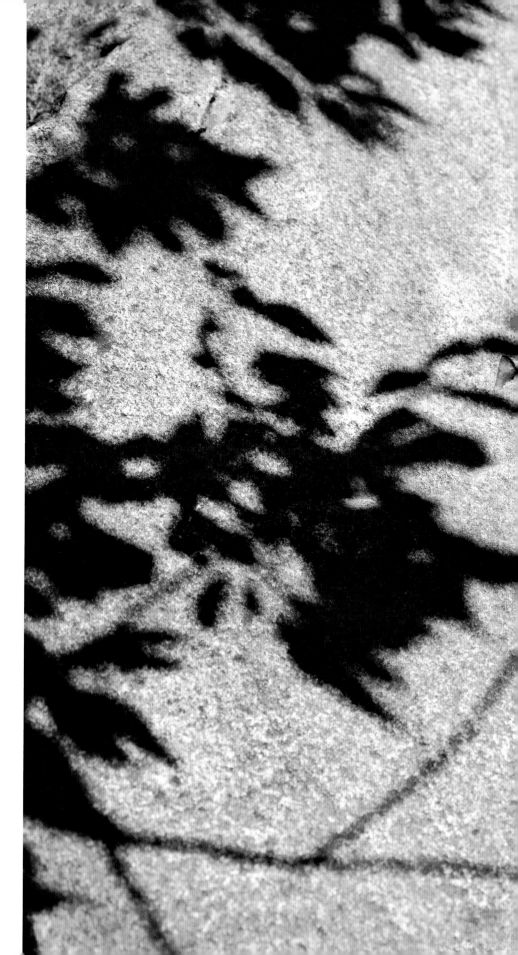

New England
Holocaust Memorial
Boston, Massachusetts, 1995

Remembrance and a call to action are at the heart of the New England Holocaust Memorial in Boston. The memorial is composed of six 54-foot glass towers. The word "Remember" is engraved in English and in Hebrew on the black granite pathway at both the memorial's entrance and its exit. Entering the towers, visitors are immediately surrounded by a fog of small white numbers—six million of them—etched into the glass, each representing a victim of the Holocaust. Beneath each tower, a steel grate covers a six-foot-deep chamber bearing the name of a concentration camp.

Historical statements and testimonials of Holocaust victims, at once deeply personal and heartbreaking, are inscribed on the base of the glass panels. Rivka Yosselevscka, a survivor who witnessed the murder of her family, wrote, "My younger sister went up to a Nazi soldier with one of her friends. Standing naked, embracing each other, she asked to be spared. He looked into her eyes and shot the two of them. They fell together in their embrace—my sister and her young friend." Gerda Weissman Klein's engraved memory conveys the hope and tragedy of life in the camp: "Ilse, a childhood friend of mine, once found a raspberry in the camp and carried it in her pocket all day to present to me that night on a leaf. Imagine a world in which your entire possession is one raspberry and you give it to your friend."

Author and Holocaust survivor Elie Weisel spoke at the memorial's dedication in 1995 about the relevance of the Holocaust and the importance of a public memorial, saying, "Look at these towers, passerby, and try to imagine what they really mean—what they symbolize—what they evoke. They evoke an era of incommensurate darkness, an era in history when civilization lost its humanity and humanity its soul. ... We must look at these towers of memory and say to ourselves, No one should ever deprive a human being of his or her right to dignity. No one should ever deprive anyone of his or her right to be a sovereign human being. No one should ever speak again about racial superiority. ... We cannot give evil another chance."

(OPPOSITE) *Lit from within, the six glass towers of the New England Holocaust Memorial glow at night.*

(FOLLOWING PAGES) *The six million numbers etched in the glass of the memorial towers represent lives lost in the Holocaust.*

My number is 174517.

I will carry the tattoo on my left arm until I die.

— Holocaust survivor Primo Levi, *memorial tower*

THEY CAME FIRST FOR THE COMMUNISTS,

AND I DIDN'T SPEAK UP BECAUSE I WASN'T A COMMUNIST.

THEN THEY CAME FOR THE JEWS,

AND I DIDN'T SPEAK UP BECAUSE I WASN'T A JEW.

THEN THEY CAME FOR THE TRADE UNIONISTS,

AND I DIDN'T SPEAK UP BECAUSE I WASN'T A TRADE UNIONIST.

THEN THEY CAME FOR THE CATHOLICS,

AND I DIDN'T SPEAK UP BECAUSE I WAS A PROTESTANT.

AND THEN THEY CAME FOR ME,

AND BY THAT TIME NO ONE WAS LEFT TO SPEAK UP.

—REV. MARTIN NIEMOLLER, *memorial pathway*

NATIONAL HOLOCAUST
MEMORIAL MUSEUM

Washington, D.C., 1993

(OPPOSITE) *Photos at the Holocaust memorial museum depict the now vanished Jewish community of Eishishok.*

(ABOVE) *The eternal flame is in a pit of earth taken from extermination sites in Nazi-occupied Europe.*

THE NATIONAL HOLOCAUST MEMORIAL MUSEUM IN WASHINGTON, D.C., unlike most of the city's monuments and museums, neither celebrates the values on which the United States was founded or to which it aspires nor commemorates an event that took place on American soil. Rather, it challenges visitors to face the question of how a democracy responds when human freedoms are imperiled.

In 1979 President Jimmy Carter explained in words now immortalized on one of the museum's walls why the United States needed to recognize the Holocaust with a national memorial: "Out of our memory ... of the Holocaust we must forge an unshakeable oath with all civilized people that never again will the world stand silent, never again will the world ... fail to act in time to prevent this terrible crime of genocide."

Designed by James Ingo Freed, the museum uses limestone, brick, and natural lighting in combinations that act as "resonators of memory" instead of providing literal images of the Holocaust. Visitors end their emotionally difficult and intellectually challenging experience by walking under an engraved quote, "For the dead and the living we must bear witness," into the Hall of Remembrance. Quotations from the Torah are engraved above rows of candles for the victims of the Holocaust. On one side of the room are the words of God to Cain after the murder of his brother Abel: "What have you done? Hark, thy brother's blood cries out to me from the ground!" On the other side Moses speaks to the Jewish people, who had escaped from slavery in Egypt: "I call heaven and earth to witness this day: I have put before you life and death, blessing and curse. Choose life—that you and your offspring shall live." The eternal flame draws attention to the engraved black granite beyond and a final prayer about remembrance from the Torah: "Only guard yourself and guard your soul carefully, lest you forget the things your eyes saw, and lest these things depart your heart all the days of your life, and you shall make them known to your children, and to your children's children."

IF GOD LETS ME LIVE … I SHALL NOT REMAIN INSIGNIFICANT.

I SHALL WORK IN THE WORLD AND FOR MANKIND. — ANNE FRANK, *memorial wall*

IDAHO ANNE FRANK
HUMAN RIGHTS MEMORIAL
Boise, Idaho, 2002

ANNE FRANK COULD SCARCELY HAVE CONCEIVED OF BOISE, IDAHO. Therefore it seems improbable that the author of a diary that has become among the world's most widely read books has become a symbolic fixture of this community almost 60 years after her death.

The diary recounts the more than two years Anne and her family spent in hiding from the Nazis in Amsterdam. The most famous passage, inscribed on the Idaho memorial, captures the insights of a girl struggling with the tragedy around her: "It's a wonder I haven't abandoned all my ideals, they seem so absurd and impractical. Yet I cling to them because I still believe, in spite of everything, that people are truly good at heart." Within a month of writing that, Frank and her family were captured by the Nazis and deported to concentration camps. Anne and her sister ended up at Bergen-Belsen in Germany, and both died of typhus in 1945, just weeks before the camp was liberated. Only Otto Frank survived. He returned to Amsterdam and published his daughter's diary, which would eventually appear in more than 60 languages.

In 1995 a traveling exhibit of Anne Frank's diary came to Boise. The response was tremendous: Nearly 50,000 people—5 percent of the state's population—viewed it. An organization formed and partnered with the city to raise funds to build a permanent memorial, and in 2002 the Anne Frank Human Rights Memorial opened to the public.

The memorial features a bronze statue of Anne opening the drapes of her family's hideout, while a nearby 180-foot wall is engraved with 60 quotes from around the world that celebrate human rights. The eclectic quotations, ranging from the preamble to the Declaration of Independence to the words of Mahatma Gandhi, echo Anne's idealism.

Even among the world's eminent thinkers and leaders, the words of a 13-year-old refusing to surrender to the brutality of the world stand out: "I see the world being slowly transformed into a wilderness. I hear the approaching thunder that, one day, will destroy us too. I feel the suffering of millions. And yet, when I look up at the sky, I somehow feel that everything will change for the better, that this cruelty too shall end, that peace and tranquility will return once more."

(OPPOSITE) A bronze statue of Anne Frank at the memorial bearing her name in Boise, Idaho, peeks out through the curtains of her family's hiding place.

How lovely to think
that no one need
wait a moment,
we can start now,
start slowly changing
the world!

— ANNE FRANK, *memorial wall*

*Frightened Polish-
Jewish families
surrender to Nazi
soldiers in 1943.*

OKLAHOMA CITY
NATIONAL MEMORIAL

Oklahoma City, Oklahoma, 2000

WHERE ONCE A GOVERNMENT BUILDING teemed with the activity of everyday life, now exists silent space. Oklahoma City, a heartland capital home to more than one million people, was shaken on the morning of April 19, 1995, when Timothy McVeigh, who harbored anti-government feelings, detonated a truck full of explosives, causing the Murrah Federal Building to be ripped apart. Almost 200 people were killed, and more than four times as many injured. Until the September 11, 2001, attacks, it was the deadliest act of terrorism carried out in the United States, and in 1997 President Bill Clinton authorized the creation of a permanent memorial on the site.

One enters the memorial, which was dedicated on the fifth anniversary of the bombing, through a large bronze gate bearing the inscription 9:01 above the doorway—the minute before the attack occurred. Inside the gate, on a grassy hillside, stand 168 empty chairs, one for each adult victim; 19 smaller chairs represent the children who were killed. The chairs overlook a reflecting pool that marks the footprint of the Murrah Building. The lone remaining wall of the building bears granite panels engraved with the names of the more than 800 survivors. This commemoration of those who must live with the physical and emotional repercussions of the attack is a unique aspect of the memorial. Visitors exit through another gate, this one reading 9:03 above the doorway—the symbolic end of the minute of the attack.

At the dedication, President Clinton spoke of "the silence and amazing grace of this memorial. Its empty chairs recall the mercy seat of Old Testament scripture, a place for the children of God to come for renewal and dedication. So this is a day both for remembrance and for renewal." He continued, "There are places in our national landscape so scarred by freedom's sacrifice that they shaped forever the soul of America—Valley Forge, Gettysburg, Selma. This place is such sacred ground."

MAY ALL WHO LEAVE HERE KNOW THE IMPACT OF VIOLENCE.

—EXCERPT FROM MISSION STATEMENT,
memorial wall

(OPPOSITE) Empty chairs at the Oklahoma City National Memorial symbolize the lives lost in the bombing of the Murrah Building.

(FOLLOWING PAGES) The mission statement of the Oklahoma City memorial greets visitors.

WE COME HERE

THOSE WHO WERE KILLED, THOSE WHO SU

MAY ALL WHO LEAVE HERE KN

MAY THIS MEMORIAL OFFER COMFORT,

TO REMEMBER

VIVED AND THOSE CHANGED FOREVER.

W THE IMPACT OF VIOLENCE.

TRENGTH, PEACE, HOPE AND SERENITY.

WORLD TRADE CENTER MEMORIAL

New York, New York, 2009 (projected)

THE NEW YORK CITY SKYLINE WAS FOREVER CHANGED on September 11, 2001, when terrorists used two hijacked airplanes as missiles and targeted the World Trade Center in lower Manhattan. In the days immediately following the attacks, in which more than 2,500 people lost their lives, temporary memorials sprang up throughout the city: Impromptu collections of candles and flowers were placed in public squares and parks. Murals bearing expressions of sorrow, loss, and bewilderment were affixed, along with personal mementos, to city fences, especially on those erected around the gaping wound of the World Trade Center site. A more ephemeral tribute, the 88 searchlights of the "Tribute in Light," trained twin beams of light resembling the twin towers above the skyline on the six-month anniversary of the attacks and now does so each year on September 11.

A design competition for a permanent memorial drew 5,000 entries, making it the largest such contest in history; however, the controversy that surrounded the process speaks to the power of hallowed ground and of memorial sites. Among several criteria, the selection committee required that the design "respect and enhance the sacred quality of the overall site and the space designed for the memorial," and specifically that the "footprints" of the World Trade Center's twin towers be a visible part of the memorial.

The chosen design—"Reflecting Absence," by architect Michael Arad and landscape designer Peter Walker—was conceived of as a "living park." In the words of the designers, "The memorial plaza is designed to be a mediating space; it belongs both to the city and to the memorial. Located at street level to allow for its integration into the fabric of the city, the plaza encourages the use of this space by New Yorkers on a daily basis. The memorial grounds will not be isolated from the rest of the city; they will be a living part of it."

The design features two recessed pools placed in the footprints of the fallen towers. Ramps by the pools lead to the underground memorial space, where visitors look through a falling curtain of water to the vast void of each pool. A low wall engraved with the names of the victims surrounds the pools. Flowing in a continuous stream, the names are arranged haphazardly to reflect the haphazard brutality of the

(OPPOSITE) Before September 11, 2001, the World Trade Center's twin towers soared more than a quarter-mile into the sky.

MAY THE LIVES REMEMBERED, THE DEEDS RECOGNIZED, AND THE SPIRIT REAWAKENED BE ETERNAL BEACONS...

—MEMORIAL MISSION STATEMENT, *World Trade Center site*

attacks. In the hallway connecting the two pools, an alcove has a small dais, where visitors can light a candle or leave an artifact in memory of loved ones; the small chamber opposite is meant for quiet contemplation.

Along the western edge of the site, a fissure exposes the underground slurry wall originally built to prevent the waters of the adjacent Hudson River from leaking into the foundation of the towers. Its presence magnifies the poignancy of what no longer remains. As visitors continue to descend underground to reach the interpretive center, located at bedrock, they pass the visible remains of the original foundations. Artifacts recovered from the twin towers—twisted steel beams, a crushed fire truck, and personal effects—stand at the entrance to the center.

In September 2006 an interim museum of remembrance—developed by an association of September 11 family members—opened opposite the World Trade Center site. Tribute WTC Visitors' Center's galleries tell the story of the twin towers from their construction through their destruction and its aftermath in sometimes unsettling detail: Displays include a window of one of the planes that smashed into the towers and a steel beam recovered from the wreckage. But it is the personal mementos of those who died, on a beautiful day that gave no hint of danger, that provide a heartbreaking intimacy.

(RIGHT) The "foot-prints" of the de-stroyed World Trade Center towers are an integral part of the memorial design.

(OPPOSITE) A night view of the proposed towers to be built along the east side of the World Trade Center site

AND TOMORROW, NEW YORK IS GOING TO BE HERE.
AND WE'RE GOING TO REBUILD AND WE'RE
GOING TO BE STRONGER THAN WE WERE BEFORE.

— MAYOR RUDOLPH GIULIANI, *at the September 11, 2001, press conference*

THE PENTAGON MEMORIAL

WE CLAIM THIS GROUND IN
REMEMBRANCE OF THE EVENTS OF
SEPTEMBER 11, 2001

TO HONOR THE 184 PEOPLE WHOSE
LIVES WERE LOST, THEIR FAMILIES,
AND ALL THOSE WHO SACRIFICE
THAT WE MAY LIVE IN FREEDOM

WE WILL NEVER FORGET

PENTAGON MEMORIAL
Arlington, Virginia, 2008 (projected)

ALTHOUGH THE MAJORITY OF THE ALMOST 3,000 PEOPLE who lost their lives on September 11, 2001, were at or near New York City's World Trade Center, 184 people died when a hijacked airplane, originally en route to Los Angeles from Washington, D.C., smashed into the Pentagon, penetrating three rings of the heavily fortified military complex. The building was fully renovated within a year, all trace of the attack erased save for a small powerful reminder: A stone, charred from the jet fuel-fed fires and bearing the date September 11, 2001, is set into the building at the point of impact. The names of those killed are etched on acrylic panels in the building.

In 2006 ground was broken for an evocative permanent memorial. The planned Pentagon Memorial uses symbolism much like that of the Oklahoma City Memorial to convey the magnitude of loss. Covering nearly two acres on the Pentagon's west side and set among maple trees, the memorial park features 184 illuminated benches, each inscribed with the name of a victim. The benches are arranged according to the victims' ages—which ranged from 3 years to 71—and locations at the time of the attack, placing them either facing the Pentagon or the sky.

(BELOW) An artist's rendering of the proposed Pentagon Memorial's 184 cantilevered benches

(OPPOSITE) A piece of marble salvaged from the wreckage at the Pentagon was unveiled at the memorial's groundbreaking, five years after the attack.

FLIGHT 93 NATIONAL MEMORIAL

Somerset County, Pennsylvania, 2011 (projected)

(BELOW) An artist's rendering of the walkway leading to the Bowl—the site of Flight 93's crash

(FOLLOWING PAGES) Almost immediately after the crash, local officials and volunteers created a temporary memorial near the crash site.

THE FLIGHT 93 MEMORIAL MOURNS what took place on September 11, 2001, and celebrates what did not. For as the twin towers of the World Trade Center fell and the Pentagon burned in the wake of terrorist attacks, above the rugged terrain of southwestern Pennsylvania, 33 passengers and 7 crew members on an airplane headed to San Francisco from New Jersey overpowered the hijackers who had commandeered the plane, preventing an attack on the U.S. Capitol or possibly the White House, and lost their own lives in the process. A year later, legislation was passed for the creation of a memorial.

The proposed memorial features a large tower containing 40 wind chimes—one for each passenger and crew member. A path lined with red maple trees leads to the Bowl, an existing landform that delineates in black slate the plane's ill-fated flight path. Engraved on a glass plate overlooking the site is the memorial's mission statement, composed by the families of the victims and the memorial committee. It reads, in part: "A common field one day. A field of honor forever."

A rock dedicated by the Federal Air Marshal Service at the Flight 93 temporary memorial

MAY ALL WHO VISIT THIS PLACE REMEMBER THE COLLECTIVE ACTS OF COURAGE AND SACRIFICE OF THE PASSENGERS AND CREW, REVERE THIS HALLOWED GROUND AS THE FINAL RESTING PLACE OF THOSE HEROES, AND REFLECT ON THE POWER OF INDIVIDUALS WHO CHOOSE TO MAKE A DIFFERENCE. —*Portion of Flight 93 Memorial Mission Statement*

PERFECT UNION

Junius Brutus Stearns's 1856 painting of George Washington addressing the Continental Convention depicts a seminal event in the life of the nation.

WE THE PEOPLE OF THE UNITED STATES, IN ORDER TO FORM A MORE PERFECT
UNION, ESTABLISH JUSTICE, INSURE DOMESTIC TRANQUILITY, PROVIDE FOR
THE COMMON DEFENCE, PROMOTE THE GENERAL WELFARE, AND SECURE THE
BLESSINGS OF LIBERTY TO OURSELVES AND OUR POSTERITY, DO ORDAIN AND
ESTABLISH THIS CONSTITUTION FOR THE UNITED STATES OF AMERICA.

—*Preamble to the U.S. Constitution, Constitution Center facade*

NATIONAL CONSTITUTION CENTER

Philadelphia, Pennsylvania, 2003

DURING THE SUMMER OF 1787, 55 representatives from the newly created United States of America met at Independence Hall, where the Declaration of Independence had been signed a decade before, and devised a system of representative democracy that would change the world. They argued, compromised, and composed a Constitution that would, above all else, ensure that the new nation held the rule of law sacrosanct. Today, two blocks away and past the cracked Liberty Bell, a 21st-century museum honors this 18th-century achievement.

(OPPOSITE) The words of the Constitution's preamble are visible from blocks away.

The design of the National Constitution Center speaks to the spirit of the famous document, the prominent use of glass on the facade and the use of skylights providing—literally—transparency, the hallmark of a democracy. The preamble to the Constitution is writ large on an exterior wall, the words "We the People" visible from several blocks away.

This principle manifests itself in the concept of popular sovereignty, the power of the citizenry to elect leaders and amend the Constitution, which ensures the rule of law and defines the roles of the branches of federal government and the states. In placing no official above the law, the Constitution limits the rise of tyrants and the successful transfer of power following elections. The Bill of Rights, the first ten amendments, secures the "Blessings of Liberty" for all people, protecting civil liberties such as the freedom of speech, due process, and equal protection under the law.

The success of the Constitution depends on the will of the people to uphold its principles. As Judge Learned Hand once noted, "Liberty lies in the hearts of men and women; when it dies there, no constitution, no law, no court can save it; no constitution, no law, no court can even do much to help it."

(ABOVE) The National Constitution Center sits just blocks from where the "miracle of Philadelphia," as George Washington called it, was written.

U.S. SUPREME COURT BUILDING

Washington, D.C., 1935

ONE SEES ONLY SKY AND STONE when standing on the shallow marble steps of the U.S. Supreme Court Building. The imposing rotunda of the Capitol Building and the opulence of the Library of Congress, both nearby, appear to fade into the distance, leaving the Supreme Court to stand alone.

The Supreme Court Building's sense of solidity and permanence seems anomalous, given its circuitous route to Washington. The Court convened for the first time in 1790, meeting in the Merchants Exchange Building in New York City, then moving to Independence Hall and City Hall in Philadelphia, before settling in the Capitol Building in Washington, D.C. Finally, former President William Howard Taft, while serving as the Court's Chief Justice, persuaded Congress in 1929 to allocate funds to build a permanent home for it. A congressionally appointed committee awarded the commission to architect Cass Gilbert, who had designed the Woolworth Building in New York.

Gilbert designed a building that is consciously imposing, providing visitors with a sense that justice is not just a human endeavor decided by nine justices but is also a time-less institution. American law is built in part on this principle: The Founding Fathers made the judiciary one of the three branches of U.S. government, affirming its intrinsic impor-tance to the new nation. Gilbert recognized this imperative in his submission of the inscription Equal Justice Under Law for the building's west pediment. The Building Commission, chaired by Chief Justice Charles Evans Hughes, agreed with the sentiment, and the words were prominently engraved. Although the source of the quotation is unknown, it is thought to be an adaptation of an aspiration Thomas Jefferson articulated in his Inaugural Address: "Equal and exact justice to all men, of whatever state or persua-sion, religious or political."

Today the phrase has become more than a part of the building's design; it has become, as Jefferson had hoped, the ideological touchstone for justices of the Court in their deliber-ations. Justice Lewis Powell noted during his tenure as president of the American Bar Association: "Equal justice under law is ... perhaps the most inspiring idea of our society. It is one of the ends for which our entire legal system exists."

THE REPUBLIC ENDURES AND THIS IS THE SYMBOL OF ITS FAITH.

— CHIEF JUSTICE CHARLES EVANS HUGHES, *1932, cornerstone laying*

STATUE OF LIBERTY

New York, New York, 1886

STANDING WITH TORCH RAISED in New York Harbor, visible from both land and sea, the Statue of Liberty was a belated centennial gift from France to commemorate the founding of the United States. She is a collection of symbols: the torch of liberty held high, one foot in chains as a reminder of America's Revolutionary War to free itself from distant rule, and the tablet in her left arm inscribed with the date of the Declaration of Independence.

The themes of liberty and democracy are celebrated in the stairwell of the statue's pedestal, where green glass plaques are etched with the words of American writers

GIVE ME YOUR TIRED, YOUR POOR, YOUR HUDDLED MASSES
YEARNING TO BREATHE FREE, THE WRETCHED REFUSE OF YOUR
TEEMING SHORE. SEND THESE, THE HOMELESS, TEMPEST-TOST
TO ME, I LIFT MY LAMP BESIDE THE GOLDEN DOOR!

— EMMA LAZARUS, *brass plaque at statue's base*

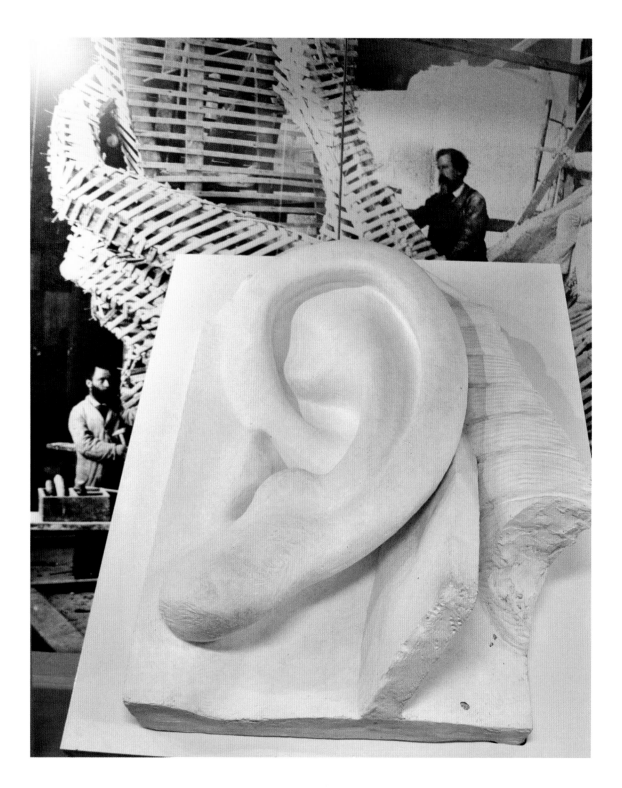

and statesmen, from Benjamin Franklin ("They that give up essential liberty to obtain a little safety deserve neither liberty nor safety") to Ralph Waldo Emerson ("For what avail the plough or sail, or land or life, if freedom fail?") to Woodrow Wilson ("I would rather belong to a poor nation that was free than to a rich nation that had ceased to be in love with liberty").

Lady Liberty symbolizes much more than freedom, however. With her proximity to Ellis Island, through which more than 12 million immigrants passed from 1892 to 1954, the statue—the Western Hemisphere's tallest structure in 1886—was a beacon to those on land or on sea. Over time the link between the statue and immigration was forged. Thus, despite all of the statue's visible symbolism, she is most closely associated with five lines of poetry engraved on a small bronze plaque deep within her base. Those lines, written in 1883 by 34-year-old poet Emma Lazarus, redefined the 300-foot icon and, in so doing, shaped the country's ideals.

(OPPOSITE) An exhibit in the statue's museum recounts Lady Liberty's storied construction.

The lines conclude "The New Colossus," a poem written in 1883 for an auction to raise funds for the construction of the statue's pedestal but not immortalized for another 20 years. Poet James Russell Lowell told Lazarus that her poem gave the statue "a raison dêtre," and in the words of New York writer Paul Auster, the sonnet "reinvented the statue's purpose, turning Liberty into a welcoming mother, a symbol of hope to the outcasts and downtrodden of the world."

Although it is a nation born of immigrants, the United States has long struggled with the concept and realities of immigration. With each generation, the country fears anew the cultural and economic impacts of recent immigrants, and xenophobic laws meet each new ethnic and racial group seeking to cross the country's borders.

(ABOVE) The Statue of Liberty museum holds a full-size replica of Lady Liberty's foot.

Lazarus's sonnet gives voice to those who seek entrance. It claims a national symbol for them and their hopes. It vividly celebrates the poorest among them—those who will face the worst of the bigotry and anger. It welcomes them and reminds those on shore of the time when their ancestors were at sea.

Give instruction unto those who cannot procure it for themselves.
CONFUCIUS

LIBRARY OF CONGRESS
Washington, D.C., 1897

T HE LIBRARY OF CONGRESS is more than a depository for books, it is a monument—a celebration of language as a means to inspire, educate, govern, and define a nation. Sentences pour from the shelves, the walls, and the ceilings. It is a grand architectural testament of, by, and for the written word.

Congress authorized the creation of a library in the 1800 act that established Washington, D.C., as the new capital of the United States. In 1814 British forces burned the Capitol Building, and with it the collection of books acquired to date. To restore the library, former President Thomas Jefferson sold Congress his personal collection of books, considered to be one of the nation's finest. The collection, reflecting his many interests, covered a range of disciplines that he argued should be available, writing, "I do not know that it contains any branch of science which Congress would wish to exclude from their collection; there is, in fact, no subject to which a Member of Congress may not have occasion to refer."

In the late 19th century, the growing collection was moved to a separate location, the newly built Jefferson Building, named for the collection's first patron. The building, an imposing granite monument of columns, archways, and a distinctive copper-domed roof, was not merely a library; its intricate Italian Renaissance architecture made it a monument to knowledge and art. As Daniel Boorstin, a historian and the former librarian of Congress, wrote of the Jefferson Building, "The glorious Library of Congress building ... is a brilliant witness to the alliance of literature and architecture against the transforming and destructive forces of time. Both architects and authors take the risks of prophecy."

The modern Library of Congress comprises several buildings and houses more than 130 million items, including more than 29 million cataloged books, and includes materials in 460 languages, as well as the world's largest collection of legal materials, films, maps, sheet music, and sound recordings. The Jefferson Building, however, remains the architectural and historical heart of the institution. The influence of ancient Greece and Rome on the decor within reflects the 19th-century reverence for classical learning. Dozens of quotations and literary allusions decorate the interior walls, citing the great authors and thinkers of Western civilization.

(OPPOSITE) The U.S. Capitol gleams through a window in the Library of Congress's Jefferson Building, above which two figures hold aloft a scroll with the words of Confucius.

The octagonal Main Reading Room is an awe-inspiring cathedral to knowledge, 160 feet from floor to ceiling of alcoves, sculptures, books, and paintings. Red marble columns soar to massive arches. A statue representing one of the eight features of civilized life and thought— philosophy, art, history, commerce, religion, science, law, and poetry—stands atop each column. Above them, angels hold tablets inscribed with quotations chosen by Charles W. Eliot, president of Harvard University from 1869 to 1909. Beneath are 104 miles of shelved books and materials—billions of words whose ideas are made manifest by the building's grandeur.

THE INQUIRY, KNOWLEDGE, AND BELIEF OF TRUTH IS THE SOVEREIGN GOOD OF HUMAN NATURE

— FRANCIS BACON, *tablet in Main Reading Room*

The 12 figures on the collar of the Main Reading Room's coffered dome represent the evolution of civilization.

WISDOM IS THE PRINCIPAL THING;
THEREFORE GET WISDOM,
AND WITH ALL THY GETTING
GET UNDERSTANDING.

—PROVERBS 4:7, *Great Hall*

In this spot stood the Wesleyan Chapel
where the First Woman's Rights Convention
in the World's history was held
July 19 and 20 1848.

Elizabeth Cady Stanton
moved this resolution
which was seconded by Frederick Douglass:
"That it is the duty of the women
of this country to secure to themselves
their sacred right
to the elective franchise"

Some of the signers of the Declaration of Rights:
Lucretia Mott · Jacob P Chamberlain · Martha C Wright · Elisha Foote
Amy Post · Charles L Hoskins · Mary Ann McClintock · Richard P Hunt
Lovina Latham · Jonathan Metcalf · Mary H Hallowell · Henry C Mott

WOMEN'S RIGHTS NATIONAL HISTORIC PARK

Seneca Falls, New York, 1980

WESLEYAN CHAPEL STANDS in ruins, behind it a long granite wall bearing the words: "When, in the course of human events, it becomes necessary for one portion of the family of man to assume among the people of the earth a position different from that which they have hitherto occupied, but one to which the laws of nature and of nature's God entitle them, a decent respect to the opinions of mankind requires that they should declare the causes that impel them to such a course." These words open the Declaration of Sentiments, a document that served as the manifesto of the women's rights movement.

In July 1848 more than 300 women and men gathered in Seneca Falls, New York, to attend the first women's rights convention, organized by Seneca Falls resident Elizabeth Cady Stanton, a major figure in the women's rights movement in the United States. They met at Wesleyan Chapel—the place of worship for former members of the Seneca Falls Methodist Church who broke with the church over its lack of support for the abolition movement—to create the intellectual framework for the movement. Over two days the group outlined its agenda and grievances and produced the Declaration of Sentiments. Structured on the Declaration of Independence, written by Thomas Jefferson less than a century earlier, the declaration enumerates injustices toward women, including being unable to vote, get a divorce, become clergy, obtain higher education, or hold property.

The declaration is not merely a collection of grievances, though; it is a call to action, and Stanton and her fellow activists spent their lives advocating for women's rights. Congress established the park in 1980 to "preserve and interpret for the education, inspiration, and benefit of present and future generations the nationally significant historical and cultural sites and structures associated with the struggle for equal rights for women."

(BELOW) A detail of the park's centerpiece: a 100-foot-long water wall engraved with the Declaration of Sentiments and its signatories.

(OPPOSITE) A plaque at the remains of Wesleyan Chapel commemorates the first women's rights convention.

(FOLLOWING PAGES) A plaque outside the remains of Wesleyan Chapel recounts the story of the women's rights convention and of the chapel in which it was held.

Wesleyan Chapel

This Chapel, site of the 1848 Women's Rights Convention, was built in 1843 by the Seneca Falls Wesleyan Methodists, a congregation dedicated to the abolition of slavery and other liberal reforms.

In 1871, the congregation sold the Chapel to a local businessman. Over the next century, a succession of commercial tenants remodeled the building many times, a process that destroyed major portions of the original structure.

In 1985, the National Park Service bought the Wesleyan Chapel and preserved its fragile remnants within a modern enclosure. The fragmented brick walls and timber roof beams are all that remain of the original Chapel, birthplace of the women's rights movement in the United States.

The 1848 Women's Rights Convention

On July 19 and 20, 1848, over 300 men and women assembled at the Wesleyan Chapel for the First Women's Rights Convention in American History.

The Convention was organized by five courageous women: Elizabeth Cady Stanton, Lucretia Mott, Martha Wright, Jane Hunt, and Mary Ann M'Clintock. Together, they drafted a Declaration of Sentiments modeled after the Declaration of Independence. They wrote that "all men and women are created equal" and enumerated specific rights, including the right to vote, denied to women solely because of their sex.

The 1848 Women's Rights Convention adopted the Declaration of Sentiments, thus inaugurating a revolutionary civil rights movement that is still in progress today.

CIVIL RIGHTS MEMORIAL
Montgomery, Alabama, 1989

I n 1988 Morris Dees, civil rights activist and founder of the Southern Poverty Law Center, made a speech in which he paid homage to the leaders of the civil rights movement. He cited activists who had been slain, among them Emmett Till, Andrew Goodman, James Chaney, Michael Schwerner, Medgar Evers, and Viola Liuzzo. Afterward, a listener asked who Evers and Liuzzo were, and Dees realized that a memorial was needed to honor and preserve the memory of those who had died in the struggle for equal rights. He contacted Maya Lin, the designer of the Vietnam Veterans Memorial. While on the plane to meet with Dees, Lin read Martin Luther King, Jr.'s "I Have a Dream" speech, with King's vow that those fighting for civil rights would not be satisfied "until justice rolls down like waters and righteousness like a mighty stream." Inspired, Lin immediately drew her vision for the memorial on an airline napkin.

The names and dates of death of those who died fighting for civil rights are etched on the Civil Rights Memorial.

Lin's design consists of two circular stone tablets—one bearing King's quote, the other the names and dates of the victims' deaths woven into a chronology of the seminal events of the movement. By intertwining the names with the movement's accomplishments, Lin sought to "illustrate the cause and effect relationships" between the sacrifices and progress, so that a "walk around the table reveals how often the act of a single person—often enough, a single death—was followed by a new and better law." By having water flow over the unpolished black granite, Lin wanted to demonstrate the power of King's metaphor as well as allow a visitor to "see and touch the names glistening in the water—and simultaneously see one's own reflection."

Several family members of the honored deceased were among those who attended the dedication ceremonies. As the dignitaries spoke, Mamie Till Mobley, the mother of a 14-year-old boy who was murdered in Mississippi in 1955 for speaking to a white woman, stood at her son's engraved name and wept, her tears becoming part of the memorial.

...UNTIL JUSTICE ROLLS DOWN LIKE WATERS
AND RIGHTEOUSNESS LIKE A MIGHTY STREAM.

MARTIN LUTHER KING JR

Water flows over the names on the Civil Right Memorial, a natural manifestation of Martin Luther King, Jr.'s words, which appear above.

MICHIGAN LABOR LEGACY LANDMARK

Detroit, Michigan, 2003

(BELOW) The grimy faces of West Virginia coal miners in 1908 are graphic testimony of the gains made by labor unions in the years since.

(OPPOSITE) The many voices of labor mingle in marble beneath the Michigan Labor Legacy arch.

LABOR UNIONS HAVE BEEN AT THE FOREFRONT of some of the key social justice efforts in the nation's history. The Michigan Labor Legacy Landmark in downtown Detroit honors labor's contributions. The hard-won victories—a 40-hour work week, medical benefits, paid holidays and sick leave, and increased salaries among them—have benefited all of society, not just union members. The memorial embodies labor craftsmanship and pride: It was funded solely by union members, and was built with union labor.

The 63-foot stainless steel arch "Transcending" emerges from the earth like "an elegantly stylized gear," according to David Barr and Sergio De Giusti, the artists who collaborated on the project. The design drew inspiration from the words of Martin Luther King, Jr., who in 1963, in a preview of his "I Have a Dream" speech that he delivered nearby,

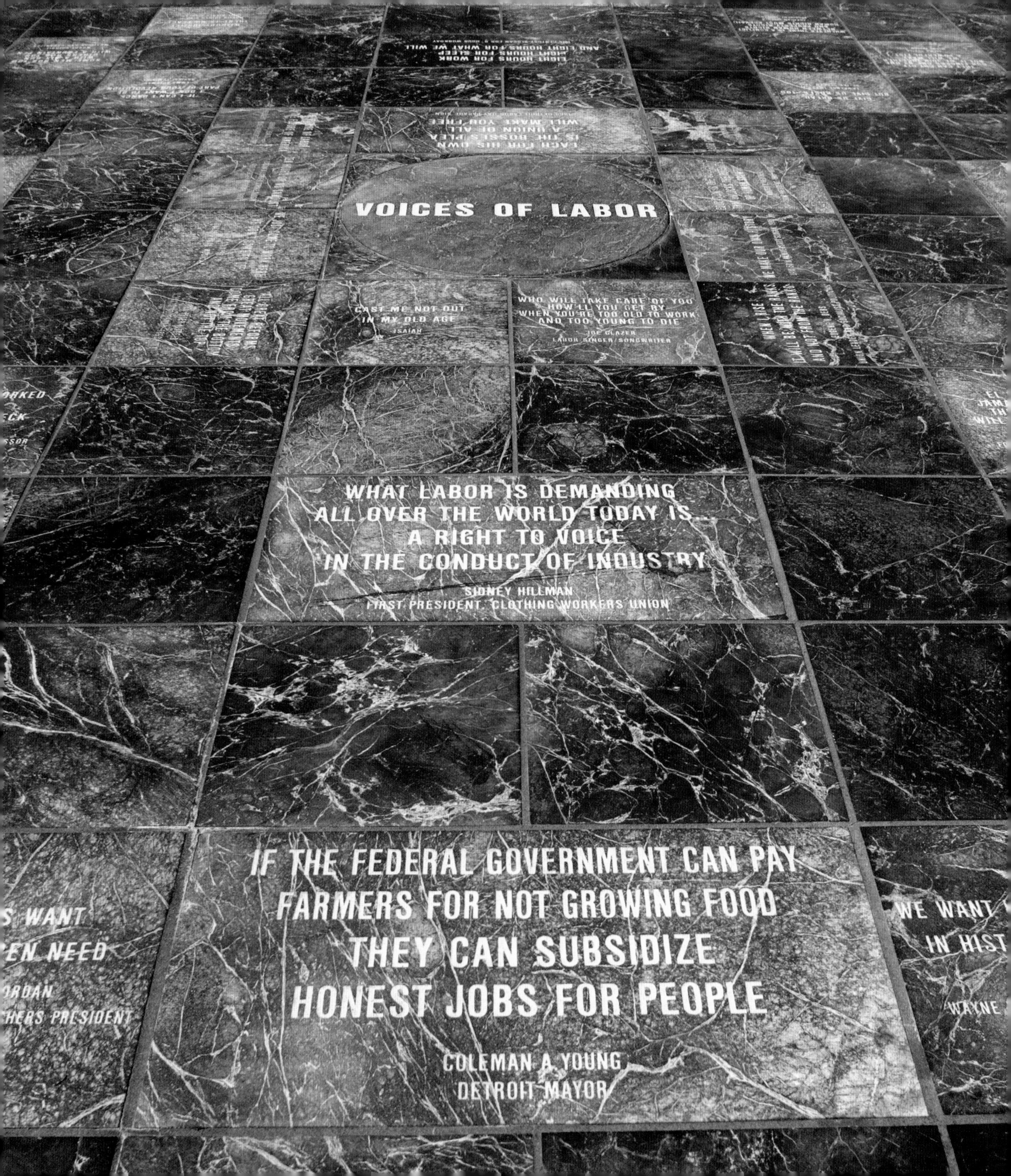

VOICES OF LABOR

CAST ME NOT OUT
IN MY OLD AGE
—ISAIAH

WHO WILL TAKE CARE OF YOU
HOW'LL YOU GET BY
WHEN YOU'RE TOO OLD TO WORK
AND TOO YOUNG TO DIE
JOE GLAZER
LABOR SINGER/SONGWRITER

WHAT LABOR IS DEMANDING
ALL OVER THE WORLD TODAY IS...
A RIGHT TO VOICE
IN THE CONDUCT OF INDUSTRY

SIDNEY HILLMAN
FIRST PRESIDENT, CLOTHING WORKERS UNION

IF THE FEDERAL GOVERNMENT CAN PAY
FARMERS FOR NOT GROWING FOOD
THEY CAN SUBSIDIZE
HONEST JOBS FOR PEOPLE

COLEMAN A. YOUNG
DETROIT MAYOR

noted that "the arc of history bends toward justice." A gap in the arch's apex represents the work still left to be done, and the light that arcs between the two sides at night symbolizes the energy of workers.

"Transcending" sits surrounded by granite boulders, upon which bronze reliefs depict themes and history relating to labor. Several tiles set into a marble pathway highlight the achievements of labor; others feature quotes relating to labor and social justice, the words chosen for their ability to remind, educate, and inspire. Included are Abraham Lincoln's "Whenever there is a conflict between human rights and property rights, human rights must prevail" and President Franklin Roosevelt's observation: "If I went to work in a factory the first thing I'd do is join a union."

Today, although the labor movement struggles with declining numbers, the concept of collective action remains an important legacy for future generations of workers. On an adjacent stone the words of union organizer and folk hero Joe Hill urge: "Don't mourn. Organize."

WE WANT MORE SCHOOLHOUSES

AND LESS JAILS…

MORE JUSTICE

AND LESS REVENGE.

— LABOR LEADER SAMUEL GOMPERS,
marble pathway

TRIBUNE TOWER

Chicago, Illinois, 1925

THE TRIBUNE TOWER, home to the *Chicago Tribune* newspaper, is the product of an international competition held in 1922 for "the most beautiful and distinctive office building in the world." It was an audacious statement and goal, but it fit the personality of the *Tribune's* owner, Col. Robert McCormick, as well as that of Chicago, which was aiming to establish itself as one of America's great cities. Out of 263 submissions, the first-place prize of $50,000 was awarded to the Gothic design of John Mead Howell and Raymond Hood: a 36-story soaring edifice with ornate masonry. Sitting just north of the Chicago River, the building now serves as the landmark entry point for North Michigan Avenue.

The tower's architecturally remarkable elements extend beyond the building's facade: Thousands of distinctive decorations are incorporated, inside and out. The building's base features more than 120 stones from famous sites around the world, including the Great Pyramid in Egypt, Notre Dame Cathedral in Paris, Westminster Abbey in England, and the Great Wall of China.

A GOOD NEWSPAPER, I SUPPOSE, IS A NATION TALKING TO ITSELF.

— ARTHUR MILLER, *Tribune Tower lobby*

In the entrance area, McCormick created a Hall of Inscriptions to serve, as *Chicago Tribune* architecture critic Blair Kamin writes, "as a secular shrine that celebrates ideals and obligations of a free press." Dozens of quotations, nearly all reportedly personally approved by McCormick, line the granite walls, including James Madison's observation: "To the press alone, checkered as it is with abuses, the world is indebted for all the triumphs which have been gained by reason and humanity over error and oppression." The First Amendment adorns the west wall, while a quotation from the Gospel of Saint John can be found on the south wall.

On the 150th anniversary of the newspaper, the Tribune Company restored the Nathan Hale Lobby and carved six new quotations into the marble walls. Writing about the role of the inscriptions, Kamin wrote, "Few products are as perishable as newspapers, but in the Tribune Tower's main lobby ... newspapers—or more precisely, powerful statements about them—become as permanent as stone. ... these quotations give monumental expression to the ideal of freedom of the press."

Give me Liberty to know, to utter and to argue freely according to my conscience, above all ❦ other liberties : Milton

AND YE SHALL
KNOW
THE TRUTH,
AND
THE TRUTH
SHALL MAKE
YOU FREE.

– JOHN 8:32,
*south wall,
Hall of Inscriptions*

*Poet John Milton's
words, carved deep
into the Tribune
Tower's facade,
champion freedom
of expression.*

Yamhill Street's quotations engage and entertain pedestrians.

YAMHILL STREET

Portland, Oregon, 1990

STAND ON YAMHILL STREET IN DOWNTOWN PORTLAND, OREGON, and you will find your-self surrounded by people who are staring at their feet and laughing out loud. The giggling people form human barricades, and soon the sidewalk is clogged, sending the normal flow of pedestrians into disarray. City officials in Portland would not have it any other way.

The culprit is a public-art project that gives an artistic dimension to a nearby city-owned parking garage. (Portland, like many cities in the United States, requires that publicly funded projects, such as parking garages, spend one percent of their costs on public art.) Streetwise—informally known around town as the Talking Sidewalk—incorporates paving stones engraved with quirky quotations into a brick sidewalk. The words and the reactions of those reading them are as much a part of the art as is the visual arrangement of the stones. Artist Bill Will conceived the idea and teamed with novelist Katherine Dunn on the project.

Their hope was to make passersby laugh, think, and pause as they went about their business. Will and Dunn selected a thousand quotations, ranging from those by Yogi Berra to Shakespeare to anonymous. Eventually, 83 sayings made the cut and were carved into stone. The pavers were placed in various directions to force the readers to move about, weav-ing through the crowds to enjoy the words.

Some of the more popular quotations include a reminder to "not step on cracks" and Marilyn Monroe's quip "I've been on a calendar but never on time." Groucho Marx's remark "I never forget a face but in your case, I'll make an exception" is engraved near Einstein's claim "Imagination is more important than knowledge."

For Will, the art is not the engraved bricks, but the public's response: "For every person who takes the time to read it, they will imagine something ... the art is in the mind of the beholder. Hopefully it stimulates their imaginations." The art is also in watching people react to the quotes, something Will admits to doing. Portland Public Art Director Eloise Damrosch says the project "engages pedestrians in a new way."

In the end, even the sidewalk itself has a sense of humor, offering William Shakespeare's lament, "You blocks, you stones, you worse than senseless things."

John F. Kennedy Center for the Performing Arts

Washington, D.C., 1971

The John F. Kennedy Center for the Performing Arts in the nation's capital speaks to the artistic soul of the city, and by extension the country. It stands as a tribute to one of its most vocal supporters. In 1958 President Dwight D. Eisenhower signed into law the National Cultural Center Act, authorizing the creation of a performing arts center, but it was his successor who truly advocated the project.

Among many mandates, the act required that the center be completely self-sustaining and privately funded. President John F. Kennedy and his wife, Jacqueline, were enthusiastic patrons of the arts, believing them critical to the well-being of society. They entertained guests at the White House with musical performances and gave interviews to popularize writers and poets. They innovated the inclusion of prominent performers, critics, composers, producers, and cultural luminaries at White House dinners, traditionally the province only of political and business leaders. The Kennedys strongly supported the center and its mission, holding fund-raisers and using their fame to promote the arts. Their dedication was unflagging; thus, after President Kennedy was assassinated in 1963, Congress chose to name the still-to-be-built arts center as a "living memorial" to Kennedy.

The Kennedy Center opened on September 8, 1971, with the debut performance of a Requiem in honor of the late President by composer Leonard Bernstein. The next morning, the New York Times wrote, "The capital of this nation finally strode into the cultural age ... with the spectacular opening of the $70 million [Kennedy Center] ... a gigantic marble temple to music, dance, and drama on the Potomac's edge." The nation's home to the arts has an aura of grandeur: long, red-carpeted hallways, elegant glass chandeliers hanging from 60-foot ceilings, sumptuous performance venues, and marble-clad facades.

Today the center's Concert Hall, Opera House, and theaters offer programs that span the artistic spectrum, and champion what Kennedy called "our contribution to the human spirit." Statements reflecting Kennedy's views on the arts line the walls of the center's River Terrace. Nowhere is his vision more apparent than in the words from his 1963 State of the Union address: "This country cannot afford to be materially rich and spiritually poor."

I LOOK FORWARD TO AN AMERICA WHICH WILL NOT BE AFRAID
OF GRACE AND BEAUTY. I LOOK FORWARD TO AN AMERICA
WHICH WILL REWARD ACHIEVEMENT IN ART AS WE REWARD
ACHIEVEMENT IN BUSINESS OR STATECRAFT. AND I LOOK
FORWARD TO AN AMERICA WHICH COMMANDS RESPECT
THROUGHOUT THE WORLD NOT ONLY FOR ITS STRENGTH
BUT FOR ITS CIVILIZATION AS WELL. AND I AM CERTAIN THAT
AFTER THE DUST OF CENTURIES HAS PASSED OVER OUR CITIES,
WE TOO WILL BE REMEMBERED NOT FOR VICTORIES OR
DEFEATS IN BATTLES OR IN POLITICS, BUT FOR OUR
CONTRIBUTION TO THE HUMAN SPIRIT.

— PRESIDENT JOHN F. KENNEDY, *Kennedy Center western wall*

TO FURTHER THE APPRECIATION OF
CULTURE AMONG ALL THE PEOPLE,
TO INCREASE RESPECT FOR THE
CREATIVE INDIVIDUAL, TO WIDEN
PARTICIPATION BY ALL THE PROCESSES
AND FULFILLMENTS OF ART—THIS
IS ONE OF THE FASCINATING
CHALLENGES OF THESE DAYS.

JOHN FITZGERALD KENNEDY

Dexter Gate at Harvard University

Cambridge, Massachusetts, 1901

(BELOW) *Charles Eliot's words above the entrance to Harvard Yard both command and entreat.*

Harvard University was established in 1636, making it the oldest institution of higher education in the country. Grounded on firm principles of education and leadership, Harvard has grown into a world-class university that has graduated seven Presidents of the United States and had more than 40 Nobel laureates on its faculty.

Charles W. Eliot, president of Harvard from 1869 to 1909, helped transform the university into the institution it is today. Eliot—whose quotations are captured on a number of

public buildings, including the Library of Congress and the Robert Gould Shaw Memorial—did not believe in education for education's sake, holding that it was necessary to train professionals and encourage public service. As he explained, "In the modern world the intelligence of public opinion is the one indispensable condition for social progress." His philosophy greatly influenced the tenor of the university and continues to be a guiding principle to matriculating students and alumni. Its essence can be found in the words on Harvard Yard's Dexter Gate, a 1901 gift to the school in memory of a former student: "Enter to grow in wisdom" greets students as they enter the university grounds. Upon leaving, they gaze on the words "Depart to serve better thy country and thy kind."

Harvard University's students receive additional inspiration as they leave the campus through Dexter Gate.

To EVERY THING THERE IS A SEASON, AND A TIME

TO EVERY PURPOSE UNDER HEAVEN.

– ECCLESIASTES 3:1, *garden path*

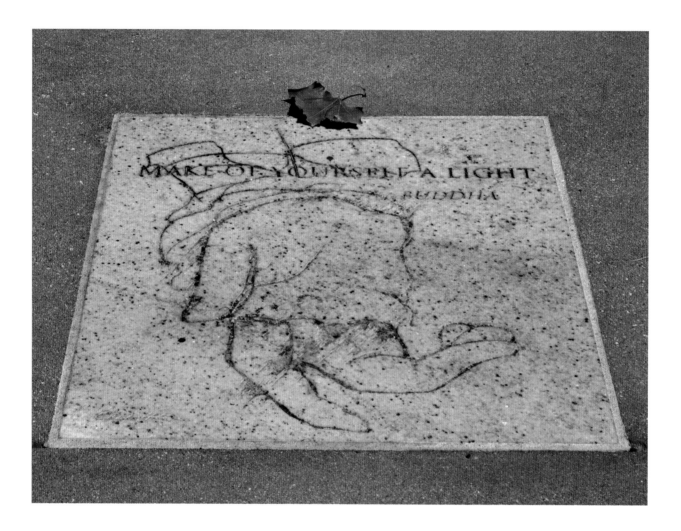

PEACE COMES WITHIN THE SOULS OF MEN

WHEN THEY REALIZE THEIR ONENESS WITH THE UNIVERSE.

— BLACK ELK, *Oglala holy man, garden path*

PALO ALTO MEDICAL FOUNDATION
Palo Alto, California, 1999

THE FOREIGN SMELLS, the rhythmic beeping of medical monitors, the awkward hushed tones of visitors—hospitals can be frightening places. At the Palo Alto Medical Foundation, the long, sterile hallways cause one's shoes to squeak with each step, and the nurses' stations hum with activity while the patients' rooms stand nearly silent, indicative of the slow, quiet pace of healing. But behind the hospital a small sun-kissed garden beckons, promising respite for patients and their families. It serves a dual function: Fresh air and sunlight offer their natural remedies, while small engraved granite tablets set in the paths offer perspective, hope, and inspiration.

Facing a public-art requirement when the hospital was built in 1999, the foundation commissioned artists Charles and Sandra Hobson to add an artistic element to the garden. David Jury, a vice president of the foundation, wanted a piece of art that would allow patients to "feel a little warmer, a little more comforting—it needed to be special." The Hobsons conceived "Human Touch," seven white speckled granite tablets engraved with Charles's line drawings of hands in all states of movement—cupped, reaching out, intertwined—coupled with healing quotations chosen by Sandra.

One stone contains a quotation from author Edith Wharton reminding readers that "There are two ways of spreading light: to be the candle or the mirror that reflects it." On a corner stone, spiritual teacher Bhagwan Shree Rajneesh advises patients and their families struggling with illness to "Be realistic, plan for a miracle."

Inspiration interplays with notions of acceptance and perseverance. Poet and writer Kahlil Gibran's observation "One may not reach the dawn save by the path of night" rests just feet from the soothing words of Ecclesiastes: "To every thing there is a season, and a time to every purpose under heaven."

Initially the tablets may seem insignificant—the engraved words and images small in comparison with the trauma occurring in the hospital—but as Julie Cameron wrote in her book *The Artist's Way,* "Art opens the closets, airs out the cellars and attics. It brings healing." Jury agrees. From a third-floor conference room he watches patients in the garden be "stopped by the words and go somewhere else for a minute."

(OPPOSITE) The words etched on granite in the Palo Alto Medical Foundation garden offer comfort while fresh air and sunlight speed the healing process.

INTERNATIONAL PEACE GARDEN
North Dakota / Manitoba, 1932

NORTH DAKOTA IS PART AND PARCEL OF THE GREAT PLAINS, with terrain varying from the rolling grasses in the east to the rugged, rocky badlands in the west, a land of temperamental weather that few would consider tranquil. Since 1956, however, it has been known as the Peace Garden State, the name proudly engraved on its license plate. Straddling the 49th parallel, the border between the United States and Canada, a parkland shared by the two countries embraces a global ideal: peace.

Canadian horticulturist Henry Moore dreamed of a garden to celebrate the enduring peace between Canada and the U.S. Proposed to a national gardening association in 1929, the idea gained support, and an interested group from North Dakota suggested an area north of Dunseith. The Depression-era Civilian Conservation Corps worked with dozens of organizations for six years to create the park, "carpet[ing] 400 acres with flowers and trees."

Today the International Peace Garden covers 2,339 acres and boasts more than 150,000 flowers, reflecting pools, miles of parkland, and several uniquely designed monuments to peace. Visitors find hope in the Peace Tower, a sculpture of four 120-foot towers symbolizing "the gathering of people from the four corners of the world." In the center of the park, directly on the border, sits the Peace Chapel. The chapel's limestone walls are engraved with dozens of quotes from around the world, each a construct for peace.

NONVIOLENCE AND TRUTH
ARE INSEPARABLE
AND PRESUPPOSE ONE ANOTHER.
THERE IS NO GOD HIGHER THAN TRUTH.

— MAHATMA GANDHI, *Peace Chapel*

Elsewhere in the garden, seven Peace Poles, a gift from the government of Japan, bear the phrase "May peace prevail" in 28 languages, and a recently installed monument composed of girders from the World Trade Center memorializes September 11.

At the 1932 dedication of the garden, a simple cairn of stones gathered from both sides of the border was unveiled. Its plaque reads: "To God and His glory / We two nations dedicate this garden / And pledge ourselves that as long / As man shall live we will not take up arms / Against one another."

DON'T WALK AHEAD OF
ME, I MAY NOT FOLLOW.
DON'T WALK BEHIND
ME, I MAY NOT LEAD.
WALK BESIDE ME, AND
JUST BE MY FRIEND.

— ALBERT CAMUS, *Peace Chapel*

The International Peace Garden's 150,000 flowers provide a vibrant contrast to the surrounding woodland.

GRAUMAN'S CHINESE THEATRE
Hollywood, California,

(BELOW) *Child actress Shirley Temple (left) and Roy Rogers's horse Trigger (right) both left their mark at Grauman's Chinese Theatre.*

(OPPOSITE) *Grauman's Theatre mixes Chinese elements and American kitsch.*

JUST AS THE PETROGLYPHS AT NEWSPAPER ROCK in New Mexico provide evidence of humanity's urge to leave a lasting impression, so does Hollywood Boulevard's Grauman's Chinese Theatre.

Built by showman Sid Grauman, the Chinese Theatre is an architectural extravaganza. Its distinctive and opulent design attracted crowds since its opening in 1927, and it is now arguably the most famous movie theater in America. The combination of Chinese elements and pure American kitsch draws attention; however, it is an addition to the original design that makes the theater such a popular destination. During the theater's construction, actress Norma Talmadge reportedly stepped in wet cement, leaving an impression of her shoe and giving Grauman a bright idea.

At the Chinese Theatre's "Forecourt to the Stars," celebrities from the entertainment industry are invited to leave their handprints and footprints in cement. The prints seem to compel people to touch them. More than two million visitors come each year, and a popular pastime for tourists is comparing their hand and shoe size with the stars'.

BIBLIOGRAPHY

GENERAL

Building Stones of Our Nation's Capital. U.S. Geological Survey, 1998.

Cambor, Kate. "Recasting the Stones," *American Prospect* (March-April 1999).

Hitt, Jack. "The American Way of Dealing with Death," New York Times, August 18, 2002.

Libeskind, Daniel, Leon Wieseltier, and Sherwin Nuland. "Monument and Memory." Columbia Seminar on Art in Society, September 27, 2002.

The National Parks: Index 2005-2007. National Park Service, 2005.

IN PRAISE OF PUBLIC LIVES

GEORGE WASHINGTON MASONIC NATIONAL MEMORIAL

Ellis, Joseph J. *His Excellency: George Washington.* Knopf, 2004.

Wills, Garry. Certain *Trumpets: The Nature of Leadership.* Simon and Schuster, 1995.

THOMAS JEFFERSON MEMORIAL

Ellis, Joseph J. *American Sphinx: The Character of Thomas Jefferson.* Random House, 1997.

LINCOLN MEMORIAL

Donald, David Herbert. *Lincoln.* Simon and Schuster, 1996.

Thomas, Christopher. *The Lincoln Memorial and American Life.* Princeton University Press, 2002.

CLEMENS CENTER

Powers, Ron. *Mark Twain: A Life.* Free Press, 2005.

THEODORE ROOSEVELT MEMORIAL

Morris, Edmund. *The Rise of Theodore Roosevelt.* Random House, 2001.

_____. *Theodore Rex.* Random House, 2002.

FRANKLIN DELANO ROOSEVELT MEMORIAL

Goodwin, Doris Kearns. *No Ordinary Time.* Simon and Schuster, 1995.

Halprin, Lawrence. *The Franklin Delano Roosevelt Memorial.* Chronicle Books, 1997.

ALBERT EINSTEIN MEMORIAL

Brian, Denis. *Einstein: A Life.* John Wiley and Sons, 1996.

JOHN F. KENNEDY PRESIDENTIAL LIBRARY

Dallek, Robert. *An Unfinished Life: John F. Kennedy, 1917-1963.* Little, Brown, 2003.

MARTIN LUTHER KING JR. INTERNATIONAL CHAPEL

Branch, Taylor. *Parting the Waters: America in the King Years, 1954-63.* Simon and Schuster, 1989.

_____. *Pillar of Fire: America in the King Years, 1963-65.* Simon and Schuster, 1999.

_____. *At Canaan's Edge: America in the King Years, 1965-68.* Simon and Schuster, 2006.

Washington, James M., ed. *A Testament of Hope: The Essential Writings and Speeches of Martin Luther King, Jr.* Harper Collins, 1986.

ROBERT F. KENNEDY MEMORIAL

Salinger, Pierre, Edwin Guthman, Frank Mankiewicz, and John Seigenthaler, eds. *"An Honorable Profession" A Tribute to Robert F. Kennedy.* Doubleday and Company, 1968.

Thomas, Evan. *Robert Kennedy: His Life.* Simon and Schuster, 2000.

ORDINARY HEROES

NEWSPAPER ROCK STATE HISTORIC PARK

Hirschmann, Fred, and Scott Thybony. *Rock Art of the American Southwest.* Graphic Arts Center Publishing Company, 1999.

Welsh, Liz, and Peter Welsh. *Rock-Art of the Southwest: A Visitor's Companion.* Wilderness Press, 2000.

MINUTE MAN NATIONAL HISTORIC PARK

Tolles, Thayer. *"The Minute Man, 1771-1775," Selections from the American Collection of the Museum of Fine Arts and the George Walter Vincent Smith Art Museum.* Springfield Library and Museums Association, 1999.

Wood, Gordon S. *The American Revolution: A History.* Random House, 2002.

ROBERT GOULD SHAW AND 54TH REGIMENT MEMORIAL

Duncan, Russell. *Where Death and Glory Meet: Colonel Robert Gould Shaw and the 54th Massachusetts Infantry.* University of Georgia Press, 1999.

GETTYSBURG NATIONAL MILITARY PARK

Hartwig, D. Scott, and Ann Marie Hartwig. *Gettysburg: The Complete Pictorial of Battlefield Monuments.* Thomas Publications, 1995.

NATIONAL D-DAY MEMORIAL

Ambrose, Stephen E. *D Day, June 6, 1944: The Climactic Battle of World War II.* Simon and Schuster, 1995.

WORLD WAR II MEMORIAL

Brinkley, Douglas, ed. *The World War II Memorial: A Grateful Nation Remembers.* Smithsonian Books, 2004.

MARINE CORPS WAR MEMORIAL

Bradley, James. *The Flags of Our Fathers.* Delacorte Press, 2001.

KOREAN WAR VETERANS MEMORIAL

Hastings, Max. *The Korean War.* Simon and Schuster, 1987.

Highsmith, Carol M., and Ted Landphair. *Forgotten No More: The Korean War Veterans Memorial Story.* Chelsea Publishing, 1995.

VIETNAM VETERANS MEMORIAL

Lin, Maya. *Boundaries.* Simon and Schuster, 2000.

UNITED STATES NAVY MEMORIAL

Alexander, John. United States *Navy Memorial: A Living Tradition.* United States Navy Foundation, 1987.

BEARING WITNESS

SALEM VILLAGE WITCHCRAFT VICTIMS' MEMORIAL

Norton, Mary Beth. *In the Devil's Snare: The Salem Witchcraft Crisis of 1692.* Knopf, 2002.

SLAVERY MONUMENT

Ferrelly, Maura. "Savannah Memorial." National Public Radio, April 30, 2001.

Morgan, Edmund S. *American Slavery, American Freedom.* W. W. Norton and Company, 2003.

ANGEL ISLAND IMMIGRATION STATION

Lai, Him Mark, Genny Lim, and Judy Yung. *Island: Poetry and History of Chinese Immigrants on Angel Island, 1910-1940.* University of Washington Press, 1999.

"In the Wooden Building: Poems From Angel Island." *Harper's Magazine* (February 2006).

CLAYTON JACKSON MCGHIE MEMORIAL

Fedo, Michael. *The Lynchings in Duluth.* Minnesota Historical Press, 2000.

Washington, Robin. "Are Lynching Memorials a Fitting Remembrance?" National Public Radio, July 3, 2006.

JAPANESE AMERICAN HISTORICAL PLAZA

Houston, Jeanne Wakatsuki, and James D. Houston. *Farewell to Manzanar.* Dell Laurel-Leaf, 1973.

Katagiri, George, and Mark Sherman, eds. *Touching the Stones: Tracing One Hundred Years of Japanese American History.* Oregon Nikkei Endowment, 1994.

NEW ENGLAND HOLOCAUST MEMORIAL

Young, James E. *The Texture of Memory: Holocaust Memorials and Meaning.* Yale University Press, 1993.

NATIONAL HOLOCAUST MEMORIAL MUSEUM

Dannatt, Adrian. *United States Holocaust Memorial Museum.* Phaidon Press, 1995.

IDAHO ANNE FRANK HUMAN RIGHTS MEMORIAL

Frank, Anne. *The Diary of Anne Frank.* Bantam, 1993.

Stahl, Amy. "Parks, Recreation & Rights." *Parks & Recreation* (December 2002).

BLACKLIST SCULPTURE GARDEN

McGilligan, Patrick, and Paul Buhle. *Tender Comrades: A Backstory of the Hollywood Blacklist.* St. Martin's Press, 1997.

Waldman, Diane, and Jenny Holzer. *Jenny Holzer.* Solomon R. Guggenheim Foundation, 2003.

OKLAHOMA CITY NATIONAL MEMORIAL

Linenthal, Edward. *The Unfinished Bombing: Oklahoma City in American Memory.* Oxford University Press, 2001.

WORLD TRADE CENTER MEMORIAL, PENTAGON MEMORIAL, AND FLIGHT 93 NATIONAL MEMORIAL

The 9/11 Commission Report: Final Report of the National Commission on Terrorist Attacks Upon the United States. W. W. Norton and Company, 2004.

A MORE PERFECT UNION

NATIONAL CONSTITUTION CENTER

Rakove, Jack N. *Original Meanings: Politics and Ideas in the Making of the Constitution.* Knopf, 1996.

U.S. SUPREME COURT BUILDING

Schwartz, Bernard. *A History of the Supreme Court.* Oxford University Press, 1995.

STATUE OF LIBERTY

Lazarus, Emma. *Emma Lazarus: Selected Poems.* Literary Classics, 2005.

Moreno, Barry. *The Statue of Liberty Encyclopedia.* New Line Press, 2000.

LIBRARY OF CONGRESS

Cole, John Y. *On These Walls: Inscriptions and Quotations in the Buildings of the Library of Congress.* Library of Congress, 1995.

Cole, John Y., and Henry Hope Reed, eds. *The Library of Congress: The Art and Architecture of the Thomas Jefferson Building.* W. W. Norton and Company, 1997.

CIVIL RIGHTS MEMORIAL

Lin, Maya. *Boundaries.* Simon and Schuster, 2000.

Williams, Juan. *Eyes on the Prize: America's Civil Rights Years, 1954-1965.* Penguin Press, 1998.

WOMEN'S RIGHTS NATIONAL HISTORIC PARK

Flexner, Eleanor. *Century of Struggle: The Woman's Rights Movement in the United States.* Belknap Press, 1996.

TRIBUNE TOWER

Kamen, Blair. *Tribune Tower: American Landmark.* Tribune Company, 2005.

Solomonson, Katherine. *The Chicago Tribune Tower Competition: Skyscraper Design and Cultural Change in the 1920s.* University of Chicago Press, 2001.

IBM SCHOOLHOUSE

Maney, Kevin. *The Maverick and His Machine: Thomas Watson, Sr., and the Making of IBM.* John Wiley, 2003.

DEXTER GATE AT HARVARD YARD

Schlesinger, Andrew. *Veritas: Harvard College and the American Experience.* Ivan R. Dee, 2005.

PALO ALTO MEDICAL FOUNDATION

Silk, Suzanne Royce. *Why I Love Books: The Artworks of Charles Hobson.* Bolinas Museum, 2002.

INTERNATIONAL PEACE GARDEN

Stormon, John. "A History of the International Peace Garden." International Peace Garden Archives, 1981.

RESOURCES

IN PRAISE OF PUBLIC LIVES

George Washington Masonic National Memorial Assn.
101 Callahan Drive
Alexandria, Virginia
(703) 683-2007
www.gwmemorial.org

Thomas Jefferson Memorial
Washington, D.C.
(202) 426-6841
www.nps.gov/thje

Lincoln Memorial
Washington, D.C.
(202) 426-6841
www.nps.gov/linc

Clemens Center
207 Clemens Center Parkway
Elmira, New York
(607) 733-5639
www.clemenscenter.com

Theodore Roosevelt Memorial
McLean, Virginia
(703) 289-2500
www.nps.gov/this

Franklin Delano Roosevelt Memorial
West Basin Drive
Washington, D.C.
(202) 426-6841
www.nps.gov/fdrm

Albert Einstein Memorial
National Academy of Sciences
2100 C Street N.W.
Washington, D.C.
(202) 334-2000
www.nasonline.org

John F. Kennedy Presidential Library
Columbia Point
Boston, Massachusetts
(866) JFK-1960
www.jfklibrary.org

Martin Luther King Jr. International Chapel
830 Westview Drive S.W.
Atlanta, Georgia
404.681.2800
www.morehouse.edu/aboutmc/chapel/index.html

Robert F. Kennedy Memorial
Arlington National Cemetery
Arlington, Virginia
(703) 607-8000
www.arlingtoncemetery.org/visitor_information/Robert_F_Kennedy.html

ORDINARY HEROES

Newspaper Rock State Historic Park
53 miles south of Moab, Utah
(435) 587-1522

www.desertusa.com/newut/du_newut_vvc.html

Minute Man National Historic Park
174 Liberty Street
Concord, Massachusetts
(978) 369-6993
www.nps.gov/mima

Robert Gould Shaw and the 54th Regiment Memorial
Boston, Massachusetts
(617) 742-5415
www.nps.gov/boaf/historyculture/shaw.htm

Gettysburg National Military Park
97 Taneytown Road
Gettysburg, Pennsylvania
717-334-1124, extension 431
www.nps.gov/gett

National D-Day Memorial
Routes 460 Bypass and 122
Bedford, Virginia
540-587-3619
www.dday.org

World War II Memorial
National Mall
Washington, D.C.
(202) 426-6841
www.nps.gov/nwwm

Marine Corps War Memorial
McLean, Virginia
(703) 289-2500
www.nps.gov/gwmp/usmc.htm

Korean War Veterans Memorial
French Drive S.W.
Washington DC
(202) 426-6841
www.nps.gov/kwvm

Vietnam Veterans Memorial
Washington, D.C.
(202) 426-6841
www.nps.gov/vive

United States Navy Memorial
701 Pennsylvania Avenue N.W.
Washington, D.C.
(800) 821-8892
www.navymemorial.org

Fire Museum of Memphis
118 Adams Street
Memphis, Tennessee
(901) 320-5650
www.firemuseum.com

National Law Enforcement Officers Memorial
400 Seventh Street N.W.
Washington, D.C.
(202) 737-3400
www.nleom

BEARING WITNESS

Salem Village Witchcraft Victims' Memorial
Danvers, Massachusetts
(978) 977-7760
http://jefferson.village.virginia
.edu/salem/danvers2.html

Slavery Monument
Riverfront
Savannah, Georgia
(877) SAVANNAH
www.savannah-visit.com

Angel Island Immigration Station
Angel Island
Marin, California
(415) 435-3972
www.angelisland.org

Clayton Jackson McGhie Memorial
310 North First Avenue West
Duluth, Minnesota
(218) 722-3186
www.claytonjackson
mcghie.org

Japanese American Historical Plaza
Tom McCall Waterfront Park
Portland, Oregon
(877) 678-5263
www.pova.org

New England Holocaust Memorial
Boston, Massachusetts
(617) 457-8755
www.nehm.org

National Holocaust Memorial Museum
100 Raoul Wallenberg Place S.W.
Washington, D.C.
(202) 488-0400
www.ushmm.org

Idaho Anne Frank Human Rights Memorial
801 South Capitol Boulevard
Boise, Idaho
(208) 345-0304
www.idaho-humanrights.org

Blacklist Sculpture Garden
823 Exposition Boulevard
Los Angeles, California
(213) 740-4561
www.fishergallery.org

Oklahoma City National Memorial
620 North Harvey Avenue
Oklahoma City, Oklahoma
(405) 235-3313
www.oklahomacity
nationalmemorial.org

World Trade Center Memorial
New York, New York
www.wtcsitememorial.org

Pentagon Memorial
100 Boundary Channel Drive
Arlington, Virginia
(703) 693-8954
http://memorial.pentagon.mil

Flight 93 National Memorial
Shanksville, Pennsylvania
(814) 443-4557
www.flight93memorial
project.org

A MORE PERFECT UNION

National Constitution Center
525 Arch Street
Philadelphia, Pennsylvania
(215) 409-6600
www.constitutioncenter.org

U.S. Supreme Court Building
One First Street N.E.
Washington, D.C.
(202) 479-3211
www.supremecourtus.gov

Statue of Liberty
New York, New York
(866) 782-8834
www.nps.gov/stli

Library of Congress
101 Independence Avenue S.E.
Washington, D.C.
(202) 707-8000
www.loc.gov

Women's Rights National Historic Park
136 Fall Street
Seneca Falls, New York
(315) 568-2991
www.nps.gov/wori

Civil Rights Memorial
400 Washington Avenue
Montgomery, Alabama
(334) 956-8200
www.tolerance.org/memorial
www.splcenter.org/crm/
memorial.jsp

Michigan Labor Legacy Landmark
Detroit, Michigan
(800) DET-ROIT
www.visitdetroit.com

Tribune Tower
435 North Michigan Avenue
Chicago , Illinois
(312) 222-3232
www.chicagotribune.com

Yamhill Street
Portland, Oregon
(877) 678-5263
www.pova.org

John F. Kennedy Center for the Performing Arts
2700 F Street N.W.
Washington, D.C.
(800) 444-1324
www.kennedy-center.org

IBM Schoolhouse
Endicott, New York
(607) 757-5355
www.ibm.com

Dexter Gate at Harvard Yard
Harvard University
Cambridge, Massachusetts
(617) 495-1551
www.harvard.edu

Palo Alto Medical Foundation
795 El Camino Real
Palo Alto, California
(650) 321-4121
www.pamf.org

International Peace Garden
North of Dunseith
North Dakota
(888) 432-6733
www.peacegarden.com

Grauman's Chinese Theatre
6925 Hollywood Boulevard
Hollywood, California
(323) 464-8111
www.manntheatres.com/
chinese

ILLUSTRATIONS CREDITS

ACKNOWLEDGMENTS

This book is dedicated to my family and in memory of my mother, Candy Coonerty. They made my life richer by generously sharing their love, support, and passion for the written word.

Writing a book on paper, although considerably easier than carving words into stone, requires the support of many people. I am deeply grateful to everyone who assisted me with this project.

My thanks to my family and friends for their enthusiasm and support throughout this effort. I owe a great debt to the amazing team at National Geographic Books led by Barbara Brownell, who made the process of making a book come to life enjoyable from start to finish. I am particularly grateful to Judith Klein at National Geographic for serving as capable and enthusiastic copy editor and sounding board.

My agent, Martha Kaplan, and the extraordinary advocate (and author) Ralph Eubanks were essential in making this book happen. I am also grateful to Cathleen Roundtree, John Seigenthaler, Marsha Scott, Ryann Collins, Paul Kalil, Elizabeth Gladden Kehoe, Rowland Rebele, Chad Cowan, Kris Reyes, Ronit Taggart, Philip Zelikow, Mary McKinley, and David Barna for their support and advice at just the right times. Zoe Elizabeth served as a wonderful reviewer of chapters, balancing criticism with praise in a way that brought out the best in the text.

I wish to express my gratitude to the Raven Society at the University of Virginia, which financially supported this project when it was still just an idea outlined on a couple of pages.

Photographer Carol M. Highsmith, whose fantastic work is properly highlighted in the book, was also a wonderful supporter when the book was just an idea, and a flexible co-worker helping to turn it into reality.

Finally, thank you Emily Bernard for living through this book with me, one comma and semicolon at a time. Your humor, support, love, enthusiasm, and copy editing skills make me the luckiest guy in the world.

INDEX

Boldface indicates illustrations.
If illustrations are included within a page span, the entire span is **boldface**.

ETCHED IN STONE
ENDURING WORDS FROM OUR NATION'S MONUMENTS
By Ryan Coonerty, Photographed by Carol M. Highsmith

Published by the National Geographic Society
John M. Fahey, Jr., President and Chief Executive Officer
Gilbert M. Grosvenor, Chairman of the Board
Nina D. Hoffman, Executive Vice President;
  President, Books Publishing Group

Prepared by the Book Division
Kevin Mulroy, Senior Vice President and Publisher
Leah Bendavid-Val, Director of Photography Publishing
  and Illustrations
Marianne R. Koszorus, Director of Design

Barbara Brownell Grogan, Executive Editor
Elizabeth Newhouse, Director of Travel Publishing
Carl Mehler, Director of Maps

Staff for this Book
Judith Klein, Editor
Jane Sunderland, Text Editor
Teresa Neva Tate, Illustrations Editor
Cinda Rose, Art Director
Meredith Wilcox, Administrative Director of Illustrations
Mike Horenstein, Production Project Manager
Cameron Zotter, Design Assistant
Connie D. Binder, Index

Rebecca Hinds, Managing Editor
Gary Colbert, Production Director

Manufacturing and Quality Management
Christopher A. Liedel, Chief Financial Officer
Phillip L. Schlosser, Vice President
John T. Dunn, Technical Director
Vincent P. Ryan, Director
Chris Brown, Director
Maryclare Tracy, Manager

Founded in 1888, the National Geographic Society is one of the largest nonprofit scientific and educational organizations in the world. It reaches more than 285 million people worldwide each month through its official journal, NATIONAL GEOGRAPHIC, and its four other magazines; the National Geographic Channel; television documentaries; radio programs; films; books; videos and DVDs; maps; and interactive media. National Geographic has funded more than 8,000 scientific research projects and supports an education program combating geographic illiteracy.

For more information, please call
1-800-NGS LINE (647-5463)
or write to the following address:

National Geographic Society
1145 17th Street N.W.
Washington, D.C. 20036-4688 U.S.A.

Visit us online at
www.nationalgeographic.com/books

For information about special discounts
for bulk purchases, please contact
National Geographic Books Special Sales:
ngspecsales@ngs.org

Library of Congress Cataloging-in-Publication Data
Etched in stone : enduring words from our nation's
monuments / by Ryan Coonerty ; photographed by
Carol M. Highsmith ; foreword by Douglas Brinkley.
    p. cm.
  Includes bibliographical references and index.
  ISBN-13: 978-1-4262-0026-7

1. National monuments—United States. 2. National
monuments—United States—Pictorial works.
3. Memorials—United States. 4. Historic sites—United
States. 5. Inscriptions—United States. 6. National
characteristics, American—Quotations, maxims, etc.
7. United States—Civilization—Quotations, maxims, etc.
8. Values—United States—Quotations, maxims, etc.
I. Title.
E159.C774 2007
973.022'2—dc22   2006031903

Printed in China.

FOUR SCORE AND SEVEN YEARS
AGO OUR FATHERS BROUGHT FORTH
ON THIS CONTINENT A NEW NATION
CONCEIVED IN LIBERTY AND DEDICA-
TED TO THE PROPOSITION THAT ALL
MEN ARE CREATED EQUAL ·

NOW WE ARE ENGAGED IN A GREAT
CIVIL WAR TESTING WHETHER THAT
NATION OR ANY NATION SO CON-
CEIVED AND SO DEDICATED CAN LONG
ENDURE · WE ARE MET ON A GREAT
BATTLEFIELD OF THAT WAR · WE HAVE
COME TO DEDICATE A PORTION OF
THAT FIELD AS A FINAL RESTING
PLACE FOR THOSE WHO HERE GAVE
THEIR LIVES THAT THAT NATION
MIGHT LIVE · IT IS ALTOGETHER FIT-
TING AND PROPER THAT WE SHOULD
DO THIS · BUT IN A LARGER SENSE
WE CAN NOT DEDICATE~WE CAN NOT
CONSECRATE~WE CAN NOT HALLOW~
THIS GROUND · THE BRAVE MEN LIV-
ING AND DEAD WHO STRUGGLED HERE